# INTERIOR FREEDOM

# INTERIOR
# FREEDOM •• Jacques Philippe

*Translated by Helena Scott*

 Scepter

Originally published as *La Liberté intérieure*
Copyright © 2002, Editions des Beatitudes, S.C.C.
Burtin, France


Scripture texts from the New and Old Testaments are taken from
The Holy Bible Revised Standard Version Catholic Edition, © 1965
and 1966 by the Division of Christian Education of the National
Council of the Churches of Christ in the United States.
All rights reserved. All copyrighted material is used by permission of
the copyright owner. No part of it may be reproduced without
permission in writing from the copyright owner.


English translation copyright © 2007,
Scepter Publishers, Inc.
P.O. Box 1391, New Rochelle, NY 10802
www.scepterpublishers.org
All rights reserved.

isbn–13: 978–1–59417-052–2

printed in the united states of america

# CONTENTS

*Refusing to suffer means refusing to live*
*Badness isn't all bad: The positive side of difficulties*
*From mastery to abandonment: Purifying the mind*
*Understanding God's will*
*"No one takes my life from me, but I lay it down of my
    own accord"*
*Helplessness in trials, and the trial of helplessness: The
    freedom of believing, hoping, and loving*

# II .. The Present Moment

# III .. The Dynamism of Faith, Hope, and Love

# IV .. From Law to Grace: Love as a Free Gift

# $\mathcal{V}$ .. Spiritual Poverty and Freedom

# INTRODUCTION

Where the Spirit of the Lord is, there is freedom.
—St. Paul [1]

We will offer God our will, our reason, our mind, our whole being through the hands and the heart of the Blessed Virgin. Then our spirit will possess that precious freedom of soul, so far removed from tension, sadness, depression, constraint, and small-mindedness. We will sail the sea of abandonment, being freed from ourselves to attach ourselves to him, the Infinite.

—Mother Yvonne-Aimée de Malestroit [2]

This book is about a basic theme of Christian life: interior freedom. Its purpose is simple. Every Christian needs to discover that even in the most unfavorable outward circumstances we possess within ourselves a space of freedom that nobody can take away, because God is its source and guarantee. Without this discovery we will always be restricted in some way, and will never taste true happiness. But if we have learned to let this inner space of freedom unfold, then, even though many things may well cause us to suffer, nothing will really be able to oppress or crush us.

[1] 2 Corinthians 3: 17.

[2] Quoted in Paul Labutte, *Une amitié voulue par Dieu* (Paris: François-Xavier de Guibert, 1999).

The thesis to be developed is a simple but very important one: we gain possession of our interior freedom in exact proportion to our growth in faith, hope, and love. This book will look specifically at how the dynamism of what are classically called the "theological virtues" is the heart of the spiritual life. It will also underline the key role of the virtue of hope in our inner growth. Hope cannot really be exercised apart from poverty of heart, so that the whole of the book may be considered a commentary on the first beatitude: "Blessed are the poor in spirit, for theirs is the kingdom of Heaven." [3]

We shall return to certain topics that have been covered in my previous books[4] and look at them more deeply: inner peace, prayer life, and docility to the Holy Spirit.

At the beginning of the third millennium, it is hoped that this book will help those who wish to open themselves to the marvelous inner renewal that the Holy Spirit wants to bring about in people's hearts, and in this way reach the glorious freedom of the children of God.

---

[3] Matthew 5: 3.

[4] *Searching for and Maintaining Peace: A Small Treatise on Peace of Heart* (New York: Alba House, 2002); *Time for God: A Guide to Prayer* (New York: Pauline Books and Media, 2005); *In the School of the Holy Spirit* (New York: Scepter, 2007).

# I

# FREEDOM AND ACCEPTANCE

## I. THE SEARCH FOR FREEDOM

Present-day culture and Christianity can, in a sense, find common ground in the concept of freedom. After all, Christianity is a message of freedom and liberation. To realize this, we need only to open the New Testament, where the words "free," "freedom," "set free" occur regularly. "The truth will make you free," says Jesus in St. John's Gospel.[1] St. Paul states: "Where the Spirit of the Lord is, there is freedom," [2] and, elsewhere, "For freedom Christ has set us free." [3] St. James calls the law of Christianity a "law of liberty." [4] What we need to do, and will try to do in the course of this book, is find out the real nature of this freedom.

Modern culture has been marked for the past few centuries by a strong aspiration for freedom. Everyone

[1] John 8: 32.
[2] 2 Corinthians 3: 17.
[3] Galatians 5: 1.
[4] James 2: 12.

11

realizes, however, how ambiguous the notion of freedom can be; false ideas of freedom have alienated people from the truth and caused millions of deaths. The twentieth century above all saw that happen, to its cost. But the desire for freedom remains observable in every sphere: social, political, economic, and psychological. Its urgency is probably due to the fact that, despite all the "progress" achieved so far, this desire still remains unfulfilled.

In the area of morality, freedom appears very nearly the only value about which people still agree unanimously at the beginning of the third millennium. Everyone more or less agrees that respect for other people's freedom is still a basic ethical norm. Undoubtedly this is more a matter of theory than practice, as western liberalism becomes progressively more totalitarian. It may be merely a manifestation of the underlying selfishness of modern man, for whom respect for the freedom of the individual is less a recognition of an ethical law than a declaration of individualism—nobody can prevent me from doing what I feel like! Yet this aspiration for freedom, so strong among people today, even though it includes a large dose of illusion and is sometimes fulfilled in mistaken ways, contains something very true and noble.

## *Freedom and happiness*

Human beings were not created for slavery, but to be the lords of creation. This is explicitly stated in the Book of

Genesis. We were not created to lead drab, narrow, or constricted lives, but to live in the wide-open spaces. We find confinement unbearable, simply because we were created in the image of God, and we have within us an unquenchable need for the absolute and the infinite. That is our greatness and sometimes our misfortune.

We have this great thirst for freedom because our most fundamental aspiration is for happiness; and we sense that there is no happiness without love, and no love without freedom. This is perfectly true. Human beings were created for love, and they can only find happiness in loving and being loved. As St. Catherine of Siena puts it,[5] man cannot live without loving. The problem is that our love often goes in the wrong direction: we love ourselves, selfishly, and end up frustrated, because only genuine love can fulfill us.

Only love, then, can satisfy us; and there is no love without freedom. The kind of love that is the result of constraint, or self-interest, or the mere satisfaction of a need, does not deserve the name love. Love is neither taken nor bought. There is true love, and therefore happiness, only between people who freely yield possession of the self in order to give themselves to one another.

Here we can get some idea of how precious freedom is. Freedom gives value to love, and love is the precondition

---

[5] "The soul cannot live without love, it always needs something to love: for it is made of love, and it is for love that I created it." *Dialogues* of St. Catherine of Siena, chapter 51.

of happiness. The reason why people attach so much importance to freedom must be because they perceive this truth, however confusedly; and from that point of view, it must be admitted they are right.

But how do we achieve the freedom that will enable love to flourish? To attain this goal, let us look first at certain widespread illusions that must be put aside if we are to enjoy true freedom.

### Freedom: Claiming autonomy or accepting dependence?

Although the idea of freedom, as we have seen, can be viewed as a meeting point between Christianity and present-day culture, it also appears paradoxically to be the point at which they are furthest apart. For modern man, to be free often means throwing off all constraint and all authority—"Neither God nor master." For Christianity, on the other hand, freedom can only be found by submitting to God, in the "obedience of faith" that St. Paul speaks of.[6] True freedom is not so much something man wins for himself; it is a free gift from God, a fruit of the Holy Spirit, received in the measure in which we place ourselves in a relationship of loving dependence on our Creator and Savior. This is where the Gospel paradox is most apparent: "Whoever would save his life will lose it, and whoever loses his life for my sake will find it." [7]

[6] Romans 1: 5.
[7] Matthew 16: 25.

In other words, people who wish to preserve and defend their own freedom at any cost will lose it, but those willing to "lose" it by leaving it trustingly in God's hands will save it. Their freedom will be restored to them, infinitely more beautiful, infinitely deeper, as a marvelous gift from God's tenderness. Our freedom is, in fact, proportionate to the love and childlike trust we have for our heavenly Father.

The living experience of the saints is there to encourage us. They gave themselves to God without reserve, wanting only to do his will. In return they received the sense of enjoying an immense freedom, which nothing in the world could take away from them, and which was the source of intense joy. How is that possible? We can try to understand it little by little.

## Outward freedom or interior freedom?

Another fundamental mistake about freedom is to make it into something external, depending on circumstances, and not something primarily internal.[8] In this field, as in so many others, we re-enact the drama experienced by St. Augustine: "You were within me, and I was outside myself, and sought you outside myself!"[9]

Let me explain. More often than not, we feel that our freedom is limited by our circumstances: the restrictions

[8] There is a very simple proof of this, which takes time to understand. As long as our sense of having greater or less freedom depends on outward circumstances, it means that we are not yet truly free.

[9] St. Augustine, *Confessions*, book 10, chap. 27.

imposed on us by society, the obligations of all kinds that other people lay upon us, this or that physical or health limitation, and so on. To find our freedom, we imagine we have to get rid of those restrictions and limitations. When we feel stifled or trapped in some way by circumstances, we resent the institutions or the people that seem to be their cause. How many grievances we have toward everything in life that doesn't go as we wish, and so prevents us from being as free as we would desire!

That way of seeing things contains a degree of truth. Sometimes certain limitations need to be remedied, restrictions overcome, in order to attain freedom. But there is also much here that is mistaken and needs to be unmasked if we are ever to taste true freedom. Even if everything we consider as preventing our freedom disappeared, that would be no guarantee that we would find the full freedom we aspire to. When we push back the boundaries, more boundaries always lie a little farther on. We risk finding ourselves forever dissatisfied. We shall always come up against painful restrictions. We can overcome a certain number, but some are inflexible: physical laws, the limitations of our human condition and of life in society, and plenty more.

## *Liberation or suicide?*

The desire for freedom that lives in the hearts of all men and women today thus often is manifested in a desperate

attempt to overcome limitations. People want to go farther, faster, to have a greater power to transform reality.
This is evident in every sphere. People think they will be
freer when biological "advances" enable them to choose
the sex of their children. They think they will find freedom in always trying to surpass their capabilities. Not
content with doing "ordinary" mountaineering, people
try "extreme mountaineering"—until the day when they
go a little too far, and the exhilarating adventure ends in a
fatal fall. This suicidal aspect of a certain kind of search
for freedom is represented very meaningfully in the
last scene of the film *The Big Blue* (*Le Grand Bleu*, directed
by Luc Besson). The hero, fascinated by the ease and
freedom of movement of dolphins in the sea, ends up
following them. The film omits to state the obvious: he
condemns himself to certain death. How many young
people have been killed by excess speed or heroin over-
doses because they aspired to freedom but never learned
the right way to it? Does that mean this aspiration is just a
dream, and we should renounce it and content ourselves
with a dull, mediocre existence? Certainly not! But we
have to discover genuine freedom inside ourselves and in
a close relationship with God.

## *"It is in your own hearts that you are restricted"*

To try to explain the nature of that inner space of freedom
that we each possess and no one can steal from us, I want

to tell you about a little experience of my own concerning St. Thérèse of Lisieux.

St. Thérèse of Lisieux has been a very dear friend of mine for many years, and I've learned an enormous amount at her school of Gospel simplicity and trust. Two years ago, I happened to be at Lisieux on one of the first occasions when her relics were to be taken from the Carmelite convent to one of the cities that had asked for them—I think it was Marseilles. The Carmelite sisters had asked the brothers of the Community of the Beatitudes for help in carrying the heavy, precious reliquary to the car that was to take it to its destination. I volunteered for this delightful job, and it gave me the unexpected chance of going into the enclosure of the Lisieux Carmel and discovering, with joy and emotion, the actual places where Thérèse lived: the infirmary, the cloister, the laundry, the garden with the chestnut-tree avenue—all places that I knew from the saint's description of them in her autobiographical writings. One thing struck me: these places were much smaller than I could have imagined. For example, at the end of her life Thérèse gives a good-humored account of the sisters dropping by to have a little chat with her on their way to make hay; but the great hayfield I had pictured to myself is in reality a mere pocket-handkerchief!

This unremarkable fact, the smallness of the places where Thérèse lived, made me think a lot. I realized what a tiny world, in human terms, she inhabited: a little provincial Carmelite convent, not outstanding for its architecture; a minuscule garden; a small community composed of religious sisters whose upbringing, education, and manners often left much to be desired; a climate where the sun shines very little . . . And she spent such a short time in the convent: ten years! However, and this is the paradox that struck me, when you read Thérèse's writings you never get the impression of a life spent in a restricted world, but just the opposite. Overlooking certain limitations in the style, her way of expressing herself and her spiritual sensitivity convey an impression of breadth, of marvelous expansion. Thérèse lives in very wide horizons, which are those of God's infinite mercy and her unlimited desire to love him. She feels like a queen with the whole world at her feet, because she can obtain anything from God, and, through love, she can travel to every point in the globe where a missionary needs her prayer and sacrifices!

There is a whole study waiting to be done on the importance of the terms used by St. Thérèse to express the unlimited dimensions of the spiritual universe she inhabits: "infinite horizons," "immense desires," "oceans of graces," "abysses of love," "torrents of mercy," and so on. Her "Manuscript B" especially, recounting her discovery of her vocation in the heart of the Church, is very revealing. Of course she speaks of suffering, the monotony of sacrifice, but all of that is overtaken and transfigured by the intensity of her inner life.

Why does Thérèse's world—humanly speaking, such a narrow and poor one—give the sense of being so ample and spacious? Why does such an impression of freedom leap out from the account she gives of her life in Carmel?

Quite simply because Thérèse loves intensely. She is on fire with love for God and charity for her sisters, and she carries the Church and the whole world with motherly tenderness. That is her secret: she is not constricted in her little convent because she loves. Love transfigures everything and touches the most banal realities with a note of infinity. All the saints have had the same experience. St. Faustina exclaims in her spiritual diary: "Love is a mystery that transforms everything it touches into beautiful things that are pleasing to God. The love of God sets the soul free. Then it is like a queen, knowing nothing of the constraints of slavery." [10]

As I reflected on this, a phrase St. Paul addressed to the Christians at Corinth came to mind: "You are not restricted by us, but you are restricted in your own hearts." [11]

Very often we feel restricted in our situation, our family, or our surroundings. But maybe the real problem lies elsewhere: in our hearts. There we are restricted, and that

[10] St. Faustina Kowalska, *Petit journal* (Marquain, Belgium: Jules Hovine), p. 319; English edition: *Diary: Divine Mercy in My Soul* (Stockbridge, Mass.: Marians of the Immaculate Conception, 1999).

[11] 2 Corinthians 6: 12.

is the root of our lack of freedom. If we loved more, love would give our lives infinite dimensions, and we would no longer feel so hemmed in.

This doesn't mean objective situations don't sometimes exist that need to be changed, or oppressive circumstances that need to be remedied before the heart can experience real interior freedom. But quite often we may also be suffering from a certain confusion. We blame our surroundings, while the real problem is elsewhere: our lack of freedom stems from a lack of love. We judge ourselves to be the victims of difficult circumstances, when the real problem (and its solution) is within us. Our heart is imprisoned by our selfishness or fears, and it is we who need to change, to learn how to love, letting ourselves be transformed by the Holy Spirit; that is the only way of escaping from our sense of confinement. People who haven't learned how to love will always feel like victims; they will feel restricted wherever they are. But people who love never feel restricted. This is what little St. Thérèse taught me. She made me understand another important thing as well, but one to be considered later: that our inability to love comes most often from our lack of faith and our lack of hope.

## *A witness for our times: Etty Hillesum*

I want to cite briefly another, more recent testimony to interior freedom, one both very different from and very close to St. Thérèse's. It moved me deeply. It is the testimony of Etty Hillesum, a young Jewish woman who died at Auschwitz in November 1943, and whose diary was published in 1981.[12] Her "story of a soul" unfolded in the Netherlands at a time when the Nazis' persecution of Jews was intensifying. When Etty began to write her journal, her moral life was far from edifying. She was emotionally vulnerable, had no fixed moral guidelines, and had had several lovers. She was, however, driven by a powerful craving for the truth about herself. Thanks to a friend of hers, a psychologist and also a Jew, she discovered (without ever becoming explicitly Christian) some of the values that lie at the heart of Christianity: prayer, the presence of God within herself, and the evangelical invitation to abandon herself trustingly to Providence. Before she was finally deported to Auschwitz, while a prisoner in a Dutch transit camp, she showed a faith in God, courage in suffering, and a devotion to neighbor that demonstrated the reality of her spirituality despite the dark areas in her life.

It is astonishing to read how this young woman devoted herself to living by the Gospel values she was discovering little by little. Just when all her exterior freedoms were being progressively taken away, she discovered within herself a happiness and interior freedom that no

---

[12] Etty Hillesum, *An Interrupted Life: The Diaries and Letters of Etty Hillesum 1941–43*, trans. A. J. Pomerans (London: Persephone Books, 1999).

one could steal from her from then on. There is a very significant passage in her spiritual experience:

This morning I cycled along the Station Quay enjoying the broad sweep of the sky at the edge of the city, breathing in the fresh, unrationed air. And everywhere signs barring Jews from the paths and the open country. But above the one narrow path still left to us stretches the sky, intact. They can't do anything to us, they really can't. They can harass us, they can rob us of our material goods, of our freedom of movement, but we ourselves forfeit our greatest assets by our misguided compliance. By our feelings of being persecuted, humiliated, oppressed. By our own hatred. By our swagger, which hides our fear. We may of course be sad and depressed by what has been done to us; that is only human and understandable. However, our greatest injury is one we inflict upon ourselves. I find life beautiful, and I feel free. The sky within me is as wide as the one stretching above my head. I believe in God and I believe in man, and I say so without embarrassment. Life is hard, but that is no bad thing. If one starts by taking one's own importance seriously, the rest follows. It is not morbid individualism to work on oneself. True peace will come only when every individual finds peace within himself; when we have all vanquished and transformed our hatred for our fellow human beings of whatever race—even into love one day, although perhaps that is asking too much. It is, however, the only solution. I am a happy person and I hold life dear indeed, in this year of Our Lord 1942, the umpteenth year of the war.[13]

## Interior freedom: Freedom to believe, hope, and love

The life experiences of St. Thérèse of Lisieux and Etty Hillesum indicate the next point we need to consider. True freedom, the sovereign liberty of Christians, resides in the possibility of believing, hoping, and loving in all circumstances, thanks to the assistance of the Holy Spirit who "helps us in our weakness."[14] Nobody can ever prevent us. "For I am sure that neither death, nor life, not angels, nor principalities, nor things present, nor things to come, nor powers, nor height, nor depth, nor anything else in all creation, will be able to separate us from the love of God in Christ Jesus our Lord."[15]

No circumstance in the world can ever prevent us from believing in God, from placing all our trust in him, from loving him with our whole heart, or from loving our neighbor. Faith, hope, and charity are absolutely free,

[13] Hillesum, *Interrupted Life*, pp. 176–77.
[14] Romans 8: 26.
[15] Romans 8: 38–39.

because if they are rooted in us deeply enough, they are able to draw strength from whatever opposes them! If someone sought to prevent us from believing by persecuting us, we always would retain the option of forgiving our enemies and transforming the situation of oppression into one of greater love. If someone tried to silence our faith by killing us, our deaths would be the best possible proclamation of our faith! Love, and only love, can overcome evil by good and draw good out of evil.

The rest of this book aims to illustrate this beautiful truth from different points of view. Whoever understands it and puts it into practice achieves sovereign freedom. Growth in faith, hope, and love is the only pathway to freedom.

Before investigating this more deeply, it is worth examining an important point that concerns the different ways of actually exercising freedom.

## *Freedom in action: Choosing or consenting?*

The mistaken idea of freedom described earlier often leads people to imagine that the only way of exercising freedom is to choose what suits them best from among various possibilities. The greater the range of choices, they think, the greater their freedom. They measure freedom by the range of options.

This idea of freedom quickly leads to dead-ends and contradictions. It is remarkably widespread, albeit subconsciously. People want to have a choice in all of life's circumstances. A choice of vacation destinations, choice of jobs, choice of the number of children they will have, and soon a choice of their children's sex and the color of their eyes. They dream of a life resembling an immense supermarket, where each aisle offers a vast assortment of possibilities and they can stroll at their ease, taking whatever they choose and leaving the rest. Or, to use another image, people would like to select their lives as they select clothes from a huge mail-order catalog.

Now, it's perfectly true that the use of freedom often involves a choice among different options. That is a good thing. But it would be completely unrealistic to see the whole question from that angle alone. There are very many quite fundamental aspects of our lives that we don't choose at all: our sex, our parents, the color of our eyes, certain aspects of our character, our mother tongue. In some respects, the elements we choose in life are far less important than the ones we don't have any choice about.

What's more, when we are adolescents our lives seem to stretch before us with a broad range of possibilities to choose from; but as time goes by, that range will get progressively narrower. We have to make choices, and the options we select reduce the number of possibilities left open. Getting married means choosing one man or one woman, thus excluding all others. (It is also worth asking in what sense people actually *choose* the person they marry—more often than not, they marry the one they fall in love with, which is not really a choice, as the word "fall" suggests! But it's no worse for that.)

I sometimes say, jokingly, that the choice of celibacy for sake of the Kingdom and the choice of Christian marriage are basically very much alike. A celibate man chooses to renounce all women, and a man who gets married renounces all women except one. That isn't really such a huge difference!

The older one gets, the fewer one's options become. "Truly, truly, I say to you, when you were young, you girded yourself and walked where you would; but when you are old, you will stretch out your hands, and another will gird you and carry you where you do not wish to go." [16] Then what will remain of our freedom, if we see it in the "supermarket" terms described earlier?

This false idea of freedom has profound repercussions on the behavior of young people today, including their approach to marriage or other forms of commitment: they put off making a final choice, because choice is perceived as a loss of freedom. Result: they don't dare to decide and never actually live! Yet life chooses for them anyway, since time passes inexorably.

[16] John 21: 18.

27

*Being free also means consenting to
what we did not choose*

The exercise of freedom as a choice among options,
plainly is important. However, to avoid making painful
mistakes we also need to understand that there is another
way of exercising freedom: less immediately exciting,
poorer, humbler, but much more common, and one im-
mensely fruitful, both humanly and spiritually. It is *consenting to what we did not originally choose.*

It is worth stressing how important this way of exercising our freedom is. The highest and most fruitful form of
human freedom is found in accepting, even more than in
dominating. We show the greatness of our freedom when
we transform reality, but still more when we accept it
trustingly as it is given to us day after day.

It is natural and easy to go along with pleasant situations
that arise without our choosing them. It becomes a problem, obviously, when things are unpleasant, go against us,
or make us suffer. But it is precisely then that, in order to
become truly free, we are often called to choose to accept
what we did not want, and even what we would not have
wanted at any price. There is a paradoxical law of human
life here: one cannot become truly free unless one accepts
not always being free!

To achieve true interior freedom we must train ourselves to accept, peacefully and willingly, plenty of things
that seem to contradict our freedom. This means consent-

ing to our personal limitations, our weaknesses, our powerlessness, this or that situation that life imposes on us, and so on. We find it difficult to do this, because we feel a natural revulsion for situations we cannot control. But the fact is that *the situations that really make us grow are precisely those we do not control.* [17] There are many examples.

## *Rebellion, resignation, consent*

Before going further it will be useful to clarify our terms. When we are faced with things that we find unpleasant or consider negative, in ourselves or in our situations, there are three possible attitudes.

The first is *rebellion.* For example, we do not accept ourselves as we are; we rebel against God who made us like this, against life that has permitted this or that event, against society, and the like. True, rebellion is not always negative—it may be an instinctive and necessary reaction in certain situations of desperate suffering; then it is a healthy reaction, provided that we do not remain fixated on it. Rebellion can also be positive as the rejection of an unacceptable situation, against which one takes action, for just motives, and using legitimate and proportionate means. What we are considering here, however, is rebel-

[17] "Man's greatest illusion is to want to have mastery over his life. . . . But life is a gift that by its very nature escapes every attempt to master it." Jean-Claude Sagne, *Viens vers le Père: L'Enfance spirituelle, chemin de guérison* (Neuilly: Editions de l'Emmanuel, 1998), p. 172.

lion as the rejection of reality. That is often our first, spontaneous reaction to difficulty or suffering. But it has never solved anything. All this sort of rebellion does is add another wrong to the existing one. It is the source of despair, violence, and resentment. A certain type of literary romanticism champions rebelliousness, but common sense tells us that nothing great or positive has ever been built upon rebellion as a rejection of reality: it only increases and spreads the wrong it aims to remedy.

Rebellion may be followed by *resignation*. We realize we cannot change this situation, or cannot change ourselves, and end up by resigning ourselves. Resignation may represent a certain degree of progress beyond rebellion, in the sense that it leads to a less aggressive and more realistic approach. But it is not enough. It may be a virtue for philosophers, but it is not a Christian virtue, since it doesn't include hope. Resignation is a declaration of powerlessness that goes no further. It may be a necessary stage, but if one stops there it also is sterile.

The attitude to aim for is *consent*. Compared with resignation, consent leads to a completely different interior attitude. We say yes to a reality we initially saw as negative, because we realize that something positive may arise from it. This hints at hope. We can, for example, say yes to what we are in spite of our failings, because we know God loves us; we trust that, out of our deficiencies, the Lord is capable of making splendid things. We can say yes to the poorest and most disappointing human raw materials, because we believe that "love is so powerful in deeds that it is able to draw good out of everything, both the good and the bad that it finds in me," as St. Thérèse of Lisieux said.[18]

The ultimate difference between resignation and consent is that with consent, even though the objective reality remains the same, the attitude of our hearts is very different. They already contain the virtues of faith, hope, and love in embryo, so to speak. For example, consenting to the deficiencies of our own being means trusting in God, who created us as we are. That act of consent, therefore, contains faith in God, confidence toward him, and hence also love, since trusting someone is already a way of loving him. Because of this presence of faith, hope, and love, consent acquires great value, scope, and fruitfulness. For wherever faith, hope, or love are, openness to God's grace, acceptance of grace, and, sooner or later, the positive effects of grace are necessarily present. Where grace is accepted, it is never in vain, but always extraordinarily fruitful.

## 2. ACCEPTING OURSELVES

### *God is realistic*

It may be that in various parts of our lives we shall have to follow the path—possibly a difficult one—that leads from

---

[18] St. Thérèse of Lisieux, Manuscrit Autobiographique A, 53 recto.

rebellion or resignation to consent, and ends finally in "choosing what we did not choose."

Let's begin with some ideas on the slow process of learning to love ourselves correctly, fully accepting ourselves just as we are. First of all, the most important thing in our lives is not so much what *we* can do as leaving room for what God can do. The great secret of all spiritual fruitfulness and growth is learning to let God act. "Apart from me, you can do nothing," [19] Jesus tells us. God's love is infinitely more powerful than anything we can do by our own wisdom or our own strength. Yet one of the most essential conditions for God's grace to act in our lives is saying yes to what we are and to the situations in which we find ourselves.

That is because God is "realistic." His grace does not operate on our imaginings, ideals, or dreams. It works on reality, the specific, concrete elements of our lives. Even if the fabric of our everyday lives doesn't look very glorious to us, only there can we be touched by God's grace. The person God loves with the tenderness of a Father, the person he wants to touch and to transform with his love, is not the person we'd have liked to be or ought to be. It's the person we are. God doesn't love "ideal persons" or "virtual beings." He loves actual, real people. He is not interested in saintly figures in stained glass windows, but in us sinners. A great deal of time can be wasted in the

[19] John 15: 5.

spiritual life complaining that we are not like this or not like that, lamenting this defect or that limitation, imagining all the good we could do if, instead of being the way we are, we were less defective, more gifted with this or that quality or virtue, and so on. Here is a waste of time and energy that merely impedes the work of the Holy Spirit in our hearts.

What often blocks the action of God's grace in our lives is less our sins or failings, than it is our failure to accept our own weakness—all those rejections, conscious or not, of what we really are or of our real situation. To "set grace free" in our lives, and paving the way for deep and spectacular changes, it sometimes would be enough to say simply "yes"—a "yes" inspired by trust in God to aspects of our lives we've been rejecting. We refuse to admit that we have this defect, that weak point, were marked by this event, fell into that sin. And so we block the Holy Spirit's action, since he can only affect our reality to the extent we accept it ourselves. The Holy Spirit never acts unless we freely cooperate. We must accept ourselves just as we are, if the Holy Spirit is to change us for the better.

Similarly, if we don't accept others—for example, if we're angry with them for not being as we want—we do not allow the Holy Spirit to act positively on our relationships or make an opportunity to change. This is a point we shall consider in more detail later.

The attitudes described are sterile. They are a refusal of reality, rooted in lack of faith in God and lack of hope, which produce a lack of love. Thus we are closed to grace, and God's action is prevented.

## *Desire for change, and consent to what we are*

Someone might object that this idea of the need to "consent to what we are," with all our deficiencies and limitations, signifies mere passivity and laziness. Should we not desire to change, to grow, to surpass ourselves in order to improve? Doesn't the Gospel invite us to conversion with the words "Be perfect, as your heavenly Father is perfect"? [20]

The desire to improve, to strive always to surpass ourselves in order to grow in perfection is obviously indispensable. There is no question of abandoning it. To stop moving forward means to stop living. Anyone who doesn't *want* to become holy never will. Ultimately, God gives us what we desire, neither more nor less. But in order to become holy, we must accept ourselves as we are. These two statements are only apparently contradictory: both things are equally necessary, because they complement and balance each other. We need to accept our limitations, but without ever resigning ourselves to mediocrity. We need to desire to change, but without ever refusing, even subconsciously, to recognize our limitations or accept ourselves.

[20] Matthew 5: 48.

The secret actually is very simple. It is to understand that we can only transform reality fruitfully if we accept it first. This also means having the humility to recognize that we cannot change ourselves by our own efforts, but that all progress in the spiritual life, every victory over ourselves, is a gift of God's grace. We will not receive the grace to change unless we desire to; but to receive the grace that will transform us, we must "receive" ourselves—to accept ourselves as we really are.

## The mediation of another's eyes

Accepting ourselves is much more difficult than it might seem. Pride, fear of not being loved, the conviction of how little we are worth, are all too deeply rooted in us. Think how badly we react to our falls, mistakes, and failures, how demoralized and upset we become, how guilty they make us feel.

Only under the gaze of God can we fully and truly accept ourselves. We need to be looked upon by someone who says, as God did through the prophet Isaiah: "You are precious in my eyes, and honored, and I love you." [21] Consider a very common experience: a girl who believes she is plain (as, curiously enough, do many girls, even pretty ones!) begins to think that she might not be so frightful after all on the day a young man falls in love

[21] Isaiah 43: 4.

with her and looks at her with the tender eyes of someone in love.

We urgently need the mediation of another's eyes to love ourselves and accept ourselves. The eyes may be those of a parent, a friend, a spiritual director; but above all they are those of God our Father. The look in his eyes is the purest, truest, tenderest, most loving, and most hope-filled in this world. The greatest gift given those who seek God's face by persevering in prayer may be that one day they will perceive something of this divine look upon themselves; they will feel themselves loved so tenderly that they will receive the grace of accepting themselves in depth.

What has just been said has an important consequence. When people cut themselves off from God, they deprive themselves of any real possibility of loving themselves.[22] This also works the other way: people who hate themselves cut themselves off from God. In *Dialogues of the Carmelites* by Georges Bernanos, the aged prioress addresses the following words to the young Blanche de la Force: "Above all, never despise yourself. It is difficult to despise ourselves without offending God in us." [23]

---

[22] This is easily seen in the developments of modern culture. When they cut themselves off from God, people end up by losing the sense of human dignity and hating themselves. It is striking, for example, to see how humor in the media is less and less the humor of tenderness and compassion, and is instead the humor of derision. Art, also, is often incapable of representing the beauty of the human face.

[23] Georges Bernanos, *Dialogues des Carmélites* (1949).

To finish with, here is a short passage from Henri Nouwen's beautiful book *The Return of the Prodigal Son*:

> For a very long time I considered low self-esteem to be some kind of virtue. I had been warned so often against pride and conceit that I came to consider it a good thing to deprecate myself. But now I realize that the real sin is to deny God's first love for me, to ignore my original goodness. Because without claiming that first love and that original goodness for myself, I lose touch with my true self and embark on the destructive search among the wrong people and in the wrong places for what can only be found in the house of my Father. [24]

## *Freedom to be sinners, freedom to become saints*

When we see ourselves with God's eyes, we experience tremendous freedom. It could be called a double freedom: to be sinners, and to become saints.

The freedom to be sinners doesn't mean we are free to sin without worrying about the consequences—that would not be freedom but irresponsibility. It means we are not crushed by the fact of being sinners—we have a sort of "right" to be poor, the right to be what we are. God knows our weaknesses and infirmities, but he is not

[24] Henri J. M. Nouwen, *The Return of the Prodigal Son: A Story of Homecoming* (London: Darton Longman and Todd, 1992), p. 107.

scandalized by them and doesn't condemn us. "As tenderly as a father treats his children, so Yahweh treats those who fear him; he knows what we are made of, he remembers that we are dust." [25] God is of course inviting us to holiness, spurring us to conversion and progress. But his gaze never makes us feel anguished at the thought of not managing. We don't feel the "pressure" that sometimes comes from other people or the way we judge ourselves, telling us we can never be good enough, making us permanently dissatisfied with ourselves and always guilty for not measuring up to some expectation or standard. That we are poor sinners doesn't mean we should feel guilty for existing, as many people may unconsciously do. God's look gives us full rights to be ourselves, with our limitations and deficiencies. It gives us the "right to make mistakes," and delivers us, so to speak, from the imprisoning sense that we ought to be something other than we are. That feeling does not originate in God's will but in our damaged psyches.

In social life we experience constant tension about meeting other people's expectations of us (or what we imagine them to be). This can become an overwhelming burden. The world has turned its back on Christianity with its dogmas and commandments, on the grounds that it is a religion of guilt. Yet there has never been a time when people were so weighed down with guilt as they are

[25] Psalm 103[102]: 14.

today. Girls feel guilty for not being as beautiful as the latest fashion model. Men feel guilty for not being as successful as the inventor of Microsoft. And so it goes. The standards of success dictated by contemporary culture weigh on us much more heavily than the appeal to perfection made by Jesus. He says to us in the Gospel: "Come to me, all you who labor and are heavy burdened, and I will give you rest. Take my yoke upon you, and learn from me, for I am meek and humble of heart. For my yoke is easy, and my burden light." [26]

Under God's gaze, we are delivered from the constraint of having to be "the best" or perpetually having to be "winners." We have a deep sense of release, because we don't have to make constant efforts to show ourselves in a favorable light or waste energy pretending to be what we are not. We can quite simply be what we are. There is no better form of "relaxation" than to rest like little children in the tenderness of a Father who loves us just as we are.

We find it so difficult to accept our own deficiencies because we imagine they make us unlovable. Since we are defective in this or that aspect, we feel that we do not deserve to be loved. Living under God's gaze make us realize how mistaken that is. Love is given freely, it's not deserved, and our deficiencies don't prevent God from loving us—just the opposite! Thus we are freed of the

[26] Matthew 11: 28–30.

terrible, despair-inducing sense that we must become "good enough" to deserve to be loved.

But while it "authorizes" us to be ourselves, the poor sinners we are, God's gaze also enables us to be supremely daring in our desire for holiness. We have the right to aspire to the summit, to aspire to the highest level of holiness, because God wants and is able to grant it. We are never imprisoned within our own mediocrity or forced into a sort of dull resignation, for we always have the hope of advancing in love. God can make us, sinners that we are, into saints: his grace can accomplish even that miracle, and we can have unlimited faith in the power of his love. Even if we fall every day, as long as we get up again and say, "Lord, thank you, because I'm sure that you will make me a saint!" we give immense pleasure to God and sooner or later will receive from him what we hope for.

The right attitude toward God, then, is having a very peaceful, very "relaxed" acceptance of ourselves and our weaknesses as well as an immense desire for holiness, and a strong determination to progress, based on limitless trust in God's grace. This double attitude is well expressed in a passage from the spiritual diary of St. Faustina:

> I desire to love You more than anyone has ever loved You before. And in spite of my wretchedness and littleness, I have my trust deeply anchored in the abyss of Your mercy, my God and my creator! In spite of my great wretchedness, I am not afraid

of anything, but I maintain the hope of singing my song of praise for ever. Let no soul doubt, even the most pitiful, so long as they are still alive, that they can become a great saint. For great is the power of God's grace.[27]

## *"Limiting beliefs" and self-prohibitions*

What has just been said will enable us to avoid the false understanding that accepting ourselves with our deficiencies means shutting ourselves up inside our limitations. Because of past injuries and past experience (someone who once told us, "You won't manage," "You'll never be any good," etc.), because of certain failures, and also because of our lack of trust in God, we have a strong tendency to carry around a whole set of "limiting beliefs" or unreal convictions that make us think we will never be capable of doing this or that, of tackling such and such a situation. There are countless examples. We tell ourselves, "I'll never manage that, I'll never get this sorted out, things will always be the same." Such sentiments have nothing to do with the consent to our own limitations we've been looking at. They are merely the result of past wounds, our fears, or our lack of trust in ourselves and in God. They must be unmasked, not clung to. In consenting to be what we are, we accept ourselves in our

[27] Sister Faustina, *Petit journal*, p. 140.

poverty but also in our richness, and that allows all our honest capacities, our true abilities, to grow and flourish. Before saying we can't do this or that, we should discern whether this estimate is the fruit of healthy spiritual realism or a purely psychological conviction that needs to be healed.

Sometimes we tend to forbid ourselves some wholesome aspiration, some accomplishment, or legitimate happiness. A subconscious psychological mechanism makes us deny ourselves happiness out of a sense of guilt or it may come from a false idea of God's will, as if we ought to deprive ourselves systematically of everything good in life! In either case, it has nothing to do with genuine spiritual realism and acceptance of our own limitations. God sometimes calls us to make sacrifices but he also sets us free from fears and false sense of imprisoning guilt. He restores to us the freedom to welcome whatever good and pleasant things he wants to give us in order to encourage and show us his tenderness.

If there is one area where nothing will ever be forbidden to us, it is holiness, provided it isn't confused with external perfection, extraordinary feats, or a permanent inability to sin. If we understand holiness properly, as the possibility of growing indefinitely in love for God and our brothers and sisters, we can be certain that nothing will be beyond our reach. All we need do is never get discouraged and never resist, but trust completely the action of God's grace.

We don't all have in us the stuff of sages or heroes. But by God's grace we do have the stuff of saints. That is the baptismal robe we put on when we received the sacrament that made us God's children.

## Accepting ourselves in order to accept other people

One other point needs considering: the deep two-way connection between acceptance of ourselves and acceptance of other people. Each strengthens the other.

Often, we fail to accept others because deep down, we do not accept ourselves. If we are not at peace with ourselves we will necessarily find ourselves at war with other people. Non-acceptance of self creates an inner tension, a sense of dissatisfaction and frustration that is then taken out on others, who become scapegoats for our inner conflict. So, for instance, when we are in a bad mood with people around us, very often it is because we are discontented with ourselves! Etty Hillesum wrote: "I have gradually come to realize that on those days when you are at odds with your neighbors you are really at odds with yourself. 'Thou shalt love thy neighbor as thyself.'" [28]

Conversely, if we close our hearts against other people, make no effort to love them as they are, never learn to be reconciled with them, we will never have the grace to

[28] Hillesum, *Interrupted Life*, p. 79.

practice the deep reconciliation with ourselves that we all need. Instead we will be perpetual victims of our own narrow-heartedness and harsh judgments toward our neighbor. This is an important point, to be developed later.

### 3. ACCEPTING SUFFERING

## Consenting to difficulties

Having looked at self-acceptance, we can now consider the acceptance of events. The basic principle is the same: we cannot change our lives effectively unless we begin by accepting them, welcoming them totally, and so consenting to all the external events that confront us.

That isn't hard in the case of what we perceive as good, pleasing, and positive. But it is hard when any kind of setback or suffering is involved. In what follows, the things we find negative are generically called "difficulties."

The subject needs to be handled carefully. It is not a matter of becoming passive and learning to endure everything, without reacting. But whatever projects we have and however well we plan them, many times situations that are beyond our control and involve a whole host of events contrary to our expectations, hopes, and desires occur, and we must accept it.

We should not limit ourselves to accepting things grudgingly, but should truly consent to them—not endure them, but in a sense "choose" them (even if in fact we have no choice, and that's what most annoys us). Choosing here means making a free act by which we not only resign ourselves but also welcome the situation. That isn't easy, especially in the case of really painful trials, but it is the right approach, and we should follow as much as possible in faith and hope. If we have enough faith in God to believe him capable of drawing good out of whatever befalls us, he will do so. "As you have believed, so let it be done to you," he says repeatedly in the Gospel.[29]

This is an absolutely fundamental truth: God can draw good out of everything, both good and bad, positive and negative. For he is God, the "Almighty Father" whom we profess in the Creed. Drawing good out of good is not so hard. But God alone, in his omnipotence, his love and his wisdom, can draw good from evil. How? No philosophy or theological argument can explain it completely. Our job is to believe it on the word of Scripture inviting us to this degree of trust: "In everything God works for good with those who love him." [30] If we believe this, we will experience it. St. Thérèse of Lisieux, rereading her autobiography a few days before her death, said: "Everything is grace."

What follows are some suggestions for entering into this attitude.

[29] E.g., Matthew 8: 13.
[30] Romans 8: 28.

### *The most painful suffering is the suffering we reject*

The worst pain of suffering lies in rejecting it. To the pain itself we then add rebellion, resentment, and the upset this suffering arouses in us. The tension within us increases our pain. But when we have the grace to accept a suffering and consent to it, it becomes at once much less painful. "Peaceful suffering is no longer suffering," said the Curé of Ars, St. Jean-Marie Vianney.

The natural thing to do in the face of suffering is to remedy it as much as we can. If we have a headache, we should take aspirin. But there will always be sufferings that have no remedies, and these we must make an effort to accept peacefully. This is not masochism or love of suffering for its own sake, but just the opposite, since consenting to suffering makes it much more bearable than tensing ourselves against it. That is true of physical suffering: a blow received in a hard, tense attitude does much more damage than one received in a relaxed attitude. Wanting to eliminate suffering at all costs can sometimes produce further sufferings that are even harder to bear. Our hedonistic society's notion that all suffering is an evil to be avoided at any price leads people to make themselves unhappy. Those who habitual seek to avoid all pain and experience only what is pleasant and comfortable, will sooner or later find themselves carrying far heavier crosses than those who try to consent to sufferings it would be unrealistic to try to eliminate.

In accepting suffering we find new strength. Scripture speaks of "the bread of tears." [31] God is faithful and always give us the strength necessary to bear, day after day, what is burdensome and difficult in our lives. Etty Hillesum said: "I now realize, God, how much You have given me. So much that was beautiful and so much that was hard to bear. Yet whenever I showed myself ready to bear it, the hard was directly transformed into the beautiful." [32]

By contrast, grace will elude us when we try to bear the additional sufferings that we heap on ourselves by refusing to consent to the ordinary trials of life.

One further point: *What really hurts is not so much suffering itself as the fear of suffering.* If welcomed trustingly and peacefully, suffering makes us grow. It matures and trains us, purifies us, teaches us to love unselfishly, makes us poor in heart, humble, gentle, and compassionate toward our neighbor. Fear of suffering, on the other hand, hardens us in self-protective, defensive attitudes, and often leads us to make irrational choices with disastrous consequences. "Man suffers most through his fear of suffering," Etty Hillesum said. The worst kind of suffering is not that which we experience; it is *represented* suffering that grips the imagination and makes us adopt false attitudes. It is not reality (basically positive, even with its share of suffering) that causes problems, but the way we imagine it and depict it.

[31] Psalm 80[79]: 5.
[32] Hillesum, *Interrupted Life*, p. 241.

## *Refusing to suffer means refusing to live*

Present-day culture, through advertising and the media, serenades us endlessly with its "gospel": avoid suffering at all costs, seek pleasure alone. It neglects to say that there is no surer way of making oneself unhappy than by doing just that. Suffering should be remedied whenever possible, but it is part of life, and attempting to get rid of it completely means suppressing life, refusing to live, and ultimately rejecting the beauty and goodness that life can bring us. "Whoever seeks to gain his life will lose it, but whoever loses his life will preserve it," [33] Jesus tells us, and his Gospel is far more reliable than the gospel of advertising. Pleasure is good and also part of life. If there were no such thing, we couldn't "give pleasure," which is the best way of showing others we love them. But pleasure is not meant to be "taken" selfishly. It is to be given and accepted. By fleeing a little suffering (the ordinary sort that would be easy to accept) people often inflict much worse suffering on themselves. For example, I have seen parents who tormented themselves for years simply because they couldn't accept a child's vocation. Rejecting the suffering of separation brought about by a life choice different from what they'd imagined, they inflicted years of unhappiness on themselves. Such examples show that the acceptance of suffering and sacrifice (when they are legitimate, of

[33] Luke 17: 33.

course) is not a masochistic, self-destructive attitude, but just the opposite. By accepting the sufferings "offered" by life and allowed by God for our progress and purification, we spare ourselves much harder ones. We need to develop this kind of realism and, once and for all, stop dreaming of a life without suffering or conflict. That is the life of heaven, not earth. We must take up our cross and follow Christ courageously every day; the bitterness of that cross will sooner or later be transformed into sweetness.

The long-term consequences of inner attitudes are more important than they might seem. When faced with daily suffering, the "burden of the day and the heat," and tiredness, we should not spend time cursing interiorly or telling ourselves we can't wait till it's over or dreaming of a different life. We should accept things as they are. Life is good and beautiful just as it is, including its burden of suffering. When God created man and woman, he laid an immense blessing on every human life, and that blessing has never been withdrawn despite sin and all its consequences: "For the gifts and the call of God are irrevocable" [34] —especially the first gift and first call, that of life itself. Every life, even when subject to pain, is infinitely blessed and valuable.

This attitude sets us firmly within reality and conserves energy otherwise wasted on complaining, wishing things

[34] Romans 11: 29.

49

were different, dreaming of an impossible world. As Christians, we can be certain that an eternity of happiness awaits us: "Everlasting joy shall be upon their faces," "and night shall be no more; they need no light of lamp or sun, for the Lord God will be their light . . ." [35] We have no true reason for complaining about the difficulties of life. Let's take to heart St. Paul's words: "This slight momentary affliction is preparing for us an eternal weight of glory beyond all comparison." [36]

## Badness isn't all bad: The positive side of difficulties

We also have to admit that difficulties, however hard they may be, bring not only disadvantages but also advantages.

The first advantage is that they prevent us from assuming exclusive ownership of our lives and our time. They prevent us from shutting ourselves up inside our programs, our plans, our wisdom. They liberate us from the prison of ourselves: our narrow-mindedness and narrowness of judgment. "As the heavens are higher than the earth, so are my ways higher than your ways, and my thoughts than your thoughts, says the Lord." [37] The worst thing that could happen would be for everything to go exactly as we wanted it, for that would be the end of any

[35] Isaiah 35: 10; Revelation 22: 5.
[36] 2 Corinthians 4: 17.
[37] Isaiah 55: 8–9.

growth. To be able to enter little by little into God's wisdom, infinitely more beautiful, richer, more fruitful, and more merciful than ours,[38] our human wisdom needs a very thorough shake-up. Not to destroy it, but to raise and purify it, and free it from its limitations. It is always marked by a certain measure of selfishness and pride, and by lacks of faith and love. Our narrow vision needs opening up to God's wisdom; we require an in-depth renewal. Sin, by its nature, is narrowing: holiness is openness of spirit and greatness of soul.

## *From mastery to abandonment: Purifying the mind*

In situations of trial, not knowing why we are being tested often is harder to bear than that testing itself. "What is the meaning?" people ask. "Why?" And they get no answer. When, by contrast, reason is satisfied, suffering is much easier to accept. It's like the doctor who hurts us— we don't get angry with him because we understand that he does it to make us better.

Let us reflect on the role of reason and mind in the spiritual life.

Like all the faculties God has endowed us with, intelligence is profoundly good and useful. Man has a thirst for truth, a need to understand, that is part of human dignity and greatness. To despise intelligence, its capacities, and

---

[38] See the hymn to God's wisdom in Romans 11: 33–36.

its role in human and spiritual life would be unjust.[39] Faith cannot do without reason; and nothing is more beautiful than the possibility given man of cooperating in the work of God by freedom, understanding, and all our other faculties. Those moments of our lives when our minds grasp what God is doing, what he is calling us to, how he is teaching us to grow, enable us to cooperate fully with the work of grace.

That is as God wants it. He did not create us as puppets but as free, responsible people, called to embrace his love with our intelligence and adhere to it with our freedom. It is therefore good and right that we want to understand the meaning of everything in our lives.

But this craving to understand everything includes certain ambiguities and needs to be purified. The motives behind our desire to understand may not always be upright. The thirst to know the truth in order to welcome it and conform our lives to it is completely in order. But there also is a desire to understand that is a desire for power: taking over, grasping, mastering the situation.

The desire may also spring from another source that is far from pure: insecurity. In this case, understanding means reassuring ourselves, seeking security in the sense that we can control the situation if we understand it. Such security is too human, fragile, deceptive—it can be wrecked from one day to the next. The only true security

---

[39] Pope John Paul II reminds us of this fact in his Encyclical *Faith and Reason* (September 14, 1998).

in this life lies in the certainty that God is faithful and can never abandon us, because his fatherly tenderness is irrevocable.

The need to understand what is happening when we are undergoing some trial is sometimes simply an expression of an inability to abandon ourselves trustingly to God and a search for human security. We must be purified of that. Full inner freedom comes from progressively freeing ourselves from the need for human security through the realization that God alone is our "rock," as Scripture says.

The liberating of intelligence from the desire for control and the need to seek security instead of abandoning ourselves to God requires that we pass through certain phases in our lives—unquestionably the most painful of all—in which we simply cannot understand the reasons for what is happening. What then? Then we must seek enlightenment by reflecting, praying, and asking the advice of appropriate people; thanks to this light, and by cooperating with what we learn, we will make progress. Yet there also are periods when we must renounce all efforts to decode the mystery. The time has come to stop our activity and abandon ourselves to God with blind trust. Light will come later. "What I am doing you do not understand now, but afterward you will understand," our Lord tells St. Peter.[40] At that stage, trying to understand at all costs would do us more harm than good. It would

[40] John 13: 7.

53

increase our suffering instead of soothing it and exacerbate our doubts, insecurity, fears, and questions without providing any answer. Then we must make acts of faith. The only thing that can bring us peace is humble and trusting prayer—the attitude expressed by the prophet Jeremiah: "It is good to wait quietly for the salvation of the Lord." [41]

### Understanding God's will

Needing to feel secure, we would like always to be sure of doing God's will. This desire to know God's will, so that we can conform ourselves to it, is normal. And usually, if we seek God's will with a sincere heart, we will receive the light to understand it. But not always. Even if we do all we can to find out God's will in this or that situation by prayer, reflection, and spiritual guidance, we will not always get a very clear answer, at least not right away.

There are two reasons for this: first, God treats us as adults, and in many situations he wants us to decide for ourselves. The second reason is purification. If we were always sure we were doing God's will and walking in the truth, we would soon become dangerously presumptuous and at risk of spiritual pride. Not always being absolutely sure we are doing God's will is humbling and painful, but it protects us. It preserves us in an attitude of constant

[41] Lamentations 3: 26.

seeking and prevents the sort of false security that would dispense us from abandoning ourselves to God.

When uncertain about God's will, it is very important that we tell ourselves: "Even if there are aspects of God's will that escape me, there are always others that I know for sure and can invest in without any risk, knowing that this investment always pays dividends." These certainties include fulfilling the duties of our state in life and practicing the essential points of every Christian vocation. There is a defect here that needs to be recognized and avoided: finding ourselves in darkness about God's will on an important question—a large-scale vocational choice or some other serious decision—we spend so much time searching and doubting or getting discouraged, that we neglect things that are God's will for us every day, like being faithful to prayer, maintaining trust in God, loving the people around us here and now. Lacking answers about the future, we should prepare to receive them by living today to the full.

## *"No one takes my life from me, but I lay it down of my own accord"*

As was said earlier, it is beneficial for us to train ourselves not only to put up with difficulties but in a certain sense to choose them. That doesn't mean provoking them! But it means that when they do arise, we accept them with all our hearts, by a positive act of freedom, impelling us to

55

move quickly from disappointment to acquiescence based on trust.

St. Thérèse of Lisieux did not like having her work interrupted. Sometimes she was asked to do work requiring quite a lot of concentration such as painting something or writing a dramatic sketch for the community. The schedule of the Carmelite community was so intense that she had very little time at her disposal. When she finally found an hour or two to devote to the job, she applied herself in the following spirit: "I choose to be interrupted." If a good Sister then came by to ask her for some little service, instead of coldly sending her away Thérèse made the effort to accept the interruption with good grace. And if nobody interrupted her, she considered that a charming present from her loving God and was very grateful to him. Whatever happened she passed the day peacefully and was never upset. In everything she could do her will, because her will was to accept everything.

Consider Jesus' words: "No one takes my life from me, but I lay it down of my own accord." [42] Here is a paradox. His life was certainly taken from him: he was put in chains, condemned, led to Calvary, and crucified. But, as the liturgy says, this was "a death he freely accepted." In his heart was deep acceptance of what his Father wanted. Jesus remained supremely free in his death, because he

[42] John 10: 18.

made it into an offering of love. By his free and loving consent, the life that was taken became a life given.

There is a shining example of this in the witness of Jacques Fesch. Arrested for murdering a policeman while pursuing a rather crazy dream (he attempted a hold-up so he could buy himself a boat and sail across the ocean), he spent three years in prison before being executed on October 1, 1957, at age 27. In his prison cell he discovered Christ and embarked on a wonderful spiritual journey. Just days before he died he wrote: "Happy are those whom God honors with martyrdom! The blood that flows is always of great worth in God's eyes, and especially the blood that is freely offered up. I'm not free myself, but if today I were offered my freedom in exchange for offending God, I'd refuse, and prefer to die. I cooperate with this execution by accepting it with all my soul, and offering it to the Lord, and so I die a little less unworthily." [43]

Our freedom always has this marvelous power to make what is taken from us—by life, events, or other people— into something offered. Externally there is no visible difference, but internally everything is transfigured: fate into free choice, constraint into love, loss into fruitfulness. Human freedom is of absolutely unheard-of greatness. It does not confer the power to change everything, but it

---

[43] Jacques Fesch, *Dans cinq heures je verrai Jésus. Journal de prison* (In five hours I will see Jesus. Prison journal) (Paris: Le Sarment-Fayard, 1989), p. 296.

does empower us to give a meaning to everything, even meaningless things; and that is much better. We are not always masters of the unfolding of our lives, but we can always be masters of the meaning we give them. Our freedom can transform any event in our lives into an expression of love, abandonment, trust, hope, and offering. The most important and most fruitful acts of our freedom are not those by which we transform the outside world as those by which we change our inner attitude in light of the faith that God can bring good out of everything without exception. Here is a never-failing source of unlimited riches. Our lives no longer have in them anything negative, ordinary, or indifferent. Positive things become a reason for gratitude and joy, negative things and opportunity for abandonment, faith, and offering: everything becomes a grace.

### *Helplessness in trials, and the trial of helplessness: The freedom of believing, hoping, and loving*

There are times in every life when we find ourselves in situations of trial and difficulty, either affecting us or someone we love. We can do nothing. However much we turn things over and examine them from every angle, there is no solution. The feeling of being helpless and powerless is a painful trial, especially when it concerns someone close to us: to see someone we love in difficulties without being able to help is one of the bitterest sufferings there is. Many parents experience it. When children are small, there is always a way of intervening, helping them. When children are older and no longer heed advice, it can be terrible for parents to see their sons or daughters turning to drugs or launching destructive love affairs. Much as they want to help, they cannot. At such times we should tell ourselves that even if we apparently have no way of intervening, we still, despite everything, can continue to believe, hope, and love. We can believe that God will not abandon our child and our prayer will bear fruit in due course. We can hope in the Lord's faithfulness and power for everything. We can love by continuing to carry that person in our heart and prayer, forgiving him and forgiving the wrong done to him; and expressing love in every way available to us, including trust, self-abandonment, and forgiveness. The more devoid of means our love is, the purer and greater it is. Even when, externally, there is nothing to be done, we still have inner freedom to continue to love. No circumstance, however tragic, can rob us of that.

For us, this should be a liberating and consoling certainty amidst the trial of powerlessness. Even if we can do nothing, as long as we believe, hope, and love, something is happening whose fruits will appear sooner or later, in the time of God's mercy. Love, though bereft of means and apparently powerless, is always fruitful. It cannot be otherwise, because it is a participation in the being and life of God. "Hope does not disappoint us, because God's

59

love has been poured into our hearts through the Holy Spirit who has been given to us." [44]

## 4. ACCEPTING OTHER PEOPLE

### *Consenting to sufferings caused by others*

Earlier we spoke of accepting difficulties with a good will instead of hardening ourselves against them. This idea can be applied to the difficulties that arise by someone else's fault. How should we react to all the sufferings caused by people around us? Our line of conduct should be exactly the same: to consent to them.

Once more it is not a question of being merely passive. Sometimes we must confront someone whose actions have made us suffer, and help him or her realize what has been done and put it right. Sometimes, too, we have a duty to react firmly against unjust situations and protect ourselves or others against harmful actions. But there will always remain a certain amount of suffering that comes from those around us and that we can neither avoid nor correct. Then we are invited to accept it with hope and forgiveness.

It is harder to accept that sort of suffering than material difficulties. A man can more easily accept missing an appointment because his car broke down than because

---

[44] Romans 5: 5.

his wife spent an hour on the telephone with a friend. We see people's freedom at work in their failings and reckon that they could have acted differently if they had wanted to.

Hard as it is, we need to learn to forgive other people for making us suffer or disappointing us, and even to accept the problems they create for us as graces and blessings. The attitude is neither spontaneous nor natural, but it is the only one by which to achieve peace and interior freedom.

## *Making allowances for differences in temperament*

When other people cause us sufferings, we should not automatically see ill will on their part, though that is what we tend to do. Many interpersonal problems, which we are quick to judge morally wrong, are simply communication difficulties and misunderstandings. Our different ways of expressing ourselves, and different psychological filters, make it hard to perceive one another's real intentions.

People have very different and sometimes conflicting temperaments and ways of seeing things, and that is something to be recognized and accepted cheerfully. Some love to have everything in order and are upset by the slightest disorder. Others feel stifled when everything is overly organized and regulated. Those who love order feel threatened by anyone who leaves the smallest object out of place; those with the opposite temperament feel they are being attacked by anyone who insists on perfect tidiness. We are quick to attach moral judgments to such behavior, calling what pleases us "good" and what doesn't "bad." Examples abound. We must be careful not to turn our families and communities into permanent war zones divided between defenders of order and defenders of freedom, partisans of punctuality and partisans of easy-goingness, lovers of peace and quiet and lovers of exuberance, early birds and night owls, chatterers and taciturn types . . . and so on. We need to accept other people just as they are, understand that their approach and values are not the same as ours, and to broaden our minds and soften our hearts toward them.[45]

That isn't easy. It means seeing our own wisdom in relative terms and becoming small and humble. We must learn to renounce the pride we take in being right, which often prevents us from entering into the other person's thoughts; and that renunciation sometimes requires a dying to ourselves that is extremely hard.

But we stand to gain everything by it. It's fortunate that other people's outlook conflicts with ours, since then we have the chance to escape our narrow-mindedness and open ourselves to other values. I have lived in a commu-

[45] This is especially important in relations between men and women. After several decades of a dominant ideology that mistook equality for sameness, and aimed for men and women to be seen as absolutely interchangeable, people are fortunately rediscovering the deep psychological differences between the sexes. See, for example, John Gray's helpful book *Men Are from Mars, Women Are from Venus* (HarperCollins, 1993).

nity for twenty-five years, and I may have received more
from people I found it hard to get along with than from
those I found congenial. Those I found hard to get along
with opened my horizons to other values, but if I'd only
met people who agreed with me, I might never have
glimpsed any new horizons.

## Some reflections on forgiveness

Of course there are cases when the suffering other people
cause us is due to a real fault on their part. The proper
attitude then is not understanding in accepting differences, but something more demanding and difficult:
forgiveness.

Modern culture doesn't rate forgiveness very highly.
More often it justifies resentment and revenge. But does
that reduce the amount of evil in the world? The only way
to diminish the suffering that burdens mankind is by
forgiveness.

> In proclaiming forgiveness and love of enemies, the
> Church is aware of adding to the spiritual heritage
> of all humanity a new mode of human relationships;
> an arduous mode, to be sure, but one that is also rich
> in hope. In this, the Church knows she can rely on
> the help of the Lord, who never abandons those
> who turn to him in times of difficulty. "Love is not
> resentful" (1 Cor 13: 5). With these words from the

First Letter to the Corinthians, the Apostle Paul recalls that forgiveness is one of the highest forms of the practice of charity. [46]

This is not the place to develop the theme of forgiveness, which is fundamental but complex. It bears repeating, however, that unless we understand the importance of forgiveness and practice it in our relations with others, we will never achieve inner freedom but will always be prisoners of our own bitterness.

When we refuse to forgive someone for harm done to us, we are adding another wrong to the first. That solves nothing at all. We are increasing the quantity of evil in the world, which has quite enough as it is. Let us not join in the propagation of evil. St. Paul tells us, "Do not be overcome by evil, but overcome evil with good." [47]

Certain things must be borne in mind if we are to remove the obstacles that make forgiveness difficult, even impossible.

### Forgiving is not the same as condoning a wrong

Sometimes we think, consciously or subconsciously, that forgiving someone who has wronged us would mean pretending they had done nothing wrong—calling bad good, or condoning an act of injustice.

[46] John Paul II, Message for Lent 2001, pp. 4–5.
[47] Romans 12: 21.

But forgiving does not mean that. Truth mustn't be mocked. Forgiving means saying: "This person has wronged me, but I don't want to condemn him; I don't want to identify him with his fault; I don't want to take justice into my own hands. God is the only one who 'searches mind and heart,' [48] and 'judges justly,' [49] and I leave it to him to weigh this person's actions and pronounce judgment. That is a difficult and delicate task that belongs to God, and I don't want to take the burden of it on myself. What's more, I don't want to pass a final judgment with no appeal on the person who has hurt me. I want to look at him with eyes of hope, because I believe something can grow and change in him, and I continue to want his good. I also believe that from the evil done to me, even if it seems irremediable from a human viewpoint, God can draw good . . ." Ultimately, we can really forgive people only because Christ rose from the dead; his Resurrection is the guarantee that God can cure every wrong and every hurt.

## *The chains of resentment*

When we forgive someone, while we are in a sense doing good to that person by canceling a debt, we are doing much good to ourselves. We rediscover a freedom that we were at risk of losing through resentment and hurt feelings.

---

[48] Revelation 2: 23.
[49] 1 Peter 2: 23.

Freedom can be diminished by overly strong attachments, by a dependence on someone whom we love too much (and in the wrong way), who becomes so indispensable to us that we partly lose our autonomy. But a refusal to forgive also binds us to the person we resent, and diminishes or destroys our freedom. We are as dependent on the people we hate as on those we love in a disproportionate manner. When we foster resentment toward someone, we can't stop thinking about him. We are filled with negative feelings that absorb a large part of our energy, and so there is an "investment" in that relationship that does not leave us available, psychologically and spiritually, for what we should be concentrating on. Resentment attacks our vital forces and does us much harm. When someone has made us suffer, our tendency is to keep the memory of the wrong alive in our minds, like a "bill" we will produce in due time to demand settlement. Those accumulated bills end up poisoning our lives. It is wiser to cancel every debt, as the Gospel invites us to. In return, we will be forgiven everything, and our hearts will be set free, whereas nurturing resentment toward others closes us to the positive things they could contribute to us.

### *"The measure you give will be the measure you get back"*

One of the more beautiful passages in the Gospel is Luke, chapter 6, verses 27–38. It is a basic text that should guide us in our attitude toward others.

Love your enemies, do good to those who hate
you. . . . [L]end, expecting nothing in return; and
your reward will be great, and you will be sons of
the Most High; for he is kind to the ungrateful and
the selfish. Be merciful, even as your Father is
merciful. Judge not, and you will not be judged;
condemn not, and you will not be condemned;
forgive, and you will be forgiven; give, and it will
be given to you; good measure, pressed down,
shaken together, running over, will be put into
your lap. For the measure you give will be the
measure you get back.

These words are very demanding, but we need to
understand the demand as a magnificent "gift" God wants
to give us. God gives what he commands, and this text
contains a promise: God can transform our hearts to the
point that they become capable of loving with a love that
is as pure, freely given, and disinterested as God's own
Love. God wants to give us the gift of forgiving as he alone
can do, and so make us like himself.

We might say the whole mystery of our redemption in
Christ, by his incarnation, his death and his resurrection,
consists of this marvelous exchange: in the heart of Christ,
God has loved us *humanly*, so as to render our human
hearts capable of loving *divinely*. God became man so that
man might become God—might love as only God is
capable of loving, with the purity, intensity, power, ten-

67

derness, and inexhaustible patience that belong to divine love.[50] It is an extraordinary source of hope and a great consolation to know that, by virtue of God's grace working in us (if we remain open to it by persevering in faith, prayer, and the sacraments), the Holy Spirit will transform and expand our hearts to the point of one day making them capable of loving as God loves.

Notice that the Gospel passage just quoted ends with one of the fundamental laws of the spiritual life—in fact of human life: "The measure you give will be the measure

[50] There is a beautiful text by St. John of the Cross about the "qualities" of divine love as the soul can experience them when transformed into love and united to God: "For when a man loves another and does him good, he does him good and loves him according to his own attributes and properties. And thus thy Spouse, being Who He is within thee, grants thee favors; for, since He is omnipotent, He does good to thee and loves thee with omnipotence; and since He is wise, thou perceivest that He does thee good and loves thee with wisdom; since He is good, thou perceivest that He loves thee with goodness; since He is holy, thou perceivest that He loves thee and grants thee favors with holiness; since He is righteous, thou perceivest that He loves thee and grants thee favors righteously; since He is merciful, compassionate, and clement, thou perceivest His mercy, compassion, and clemency; and, since His Being is strong and sublime and delicate, thou perceivest that He loves thee with strength, sublimity, and delicacy; and since He is clean and pure, thou perceivest that He loves thee with cleanness and purity; and since He is true, thou perceivest that He loves thee truly; and since He is liberal, thou knowest that He loves thee and grants thee favors with liberality, without self-interest, solely that He may do thee good; as He is the virtue of the greatest humility, He loves thee with the greatest humility, and with the greatest esteem, making thee His equal, joyfully revealing Himself to thee, in these ways, which are His knowledge, by means of this His countenance, full of graces, and saying to thee in this His union, not without great rejoicing on thy part: I am thine and for thee, and I delight to be such as I am that I may be thine and give Myself to thee." St. John of the Cross, *Living Flame of Love*, Stanza III, first line, no. 6 (translated by E. Allison Peers, London: Burns & Oates, 1935 [1977], p. 165).

you get back." On the face of it, this could simply mean that God will be generous in rewarding those who are generous in loving and forgiving, and will give a smaller reward to those whose attitude toward others has been mean. But the phrase has a deeper sense. God does not punish anyone: people punish themselves. The Gospel expresses a "law" that is part and parcel of being human: those who refuse to forgive, who refuse to love, will sooner or later be victims of their own lack of love. The evil we do to or wish on others will end up turning against us. Those who are strict with their neighbor will suffer that strictness. Our judgments, mistrust, rejection, or resentment imprison us in a net that will strangle us. Our deepest aspirations for the absolute, the infinite, will be blocked and go unfulfilled, because lack of mercy toward another has enclosed us in a world of calculation and self-interest. This is an inexorable law: "You will never get out till you have paid the last penny." [51]

Forgiveness releases us from that curse. The cancellation of debts that it brings about makes possible a relation to the other based on free give-and-take, which is essential to genuine love. And none of us can live without genuine love.

When our hearts feel cramped, very often we need seek no other reason than this: we are refusing to love and forgive generously. Generosity in love and forgiveness,

[51] Matthew 5: 26.

make us "sons of the Most High," and set us free to explore the limitless oceans of God's love and life, where the deepest aspirations of our own hearts will one day be satisfied. If you love your neighbor, Isaiah tells us, "then shall your light break forth like the dawn, and your healing shall spring up speedily . . . you shall be like a watered garden, like a spring of water, whose waters fail not." [52]

## How other people's faults can be good for us

"Badness isn't all bad." The bad behavior of those around us, which causes us suffering, offers certain benefits!

In our relations with other people we naturally seek that which we lack, and especially what we lacked in childhood. Other people's imperfections, and the disappointments they cause us, oblige us to establish a relationship with them that is not limited to an unconscious search for satisfaction of our needs, but tends to become pure and disinterested, like God's love: "Be perfect as your heavenly Father is perfect." [53]

Those imperfections also help us not to look to others for happiness, plenitude, and fulfillment we can find only in God. Thus they invite us to "take root" in God. Disappointment in a relationship with someone from whom we were expecting a lot (perhaps too much) can teach us to go deeper in prayer, in our relationship with God, and to

[52] Isaiah 58: 8, 11.
[53] Matthew 5: 48.

look to him for that fullness, that peace and security, that only his infinite love can guarantee. Disappointments in relationships with other people oblige us to pass from "idolatrous" love to a love that is realistic, free, and happy. Romantic love will always be threatened with disappointments. Charity never is, because it "does not insist on its own way" [54] or seek its own interest.

## *Other people's offenses take nothing from us*

One of the biggest obstacles to forgiving is the feeling that the other party's behavior has deprived us of something important, even vital. This confused feeling nourishes resentment. The thing in question may be material, or affective or moral (not getting the love I had a right to, or the esteem, etc.), or even spiritual (the behavior of the person at the head of my community keeps my spiritual life from developing as it should. . .).

To live at peace, even when it is the people around us who are causing us suffering, we must take a fresh, radical look at our frustration. It does not correspond to reality. Other people's faults *do not deprive us of anything*. We have no valid reason for resenting them or their actions.

On the material plane, of course, other people can deprive us of many things. But not of what is essential, the only true and lasting good: God's love for us and the love

[54] 1 Corinthians 13: 5.

we can have for him, with the inner growth it produces. Nobody can prevent us from believing in God, hoping in him, and loving him, everywhere and in all circumstances. Faith, hope, and love make human beings fully human. All else is secondary and relative; even if we are deprived of it, that is not an absolute evil. There is within us something indestructible that is guaranteed by God's faithfulness and love. "The Lord is my shepherd, I shall not want. . . Even though I walk through the valley of the shadow of death, I fear no evil: for thou art with me; thy rod and thy staff, they comfort me." [55]

Rather than wasting time and energy blaming others for what isn't working out, or reproaching them for what we think they are depriving us of, we should strive to acquire spiritual autonomy by deepening our relationship with God, the one unfailing source of all good, and growing in faith, hope, and disinterested love. That others are sinners cannot prevent us from becoming saints. Nobody really deprives us of anything. At the end of our lives, when we come face to face with God, it would be childish to blame others for our lack of spiritual progress.

## The trap of indifference

Sometimes we are particularly worried about things that are not going well around us, in our community,

[55] Psalm 23[22]: 1, 4.

our family, or our church circle. We are tempted to get discouraged and give up. That is when we have to tell ourselves: whatever happens, whatever mistakes and faults are committed by this person or that, *it robs us of exactly nothing*. Even though we lived among people who were committing mortal sins from morning till night, that could not prevent us from loving God and serving our neighbor, or deprive us of any spiritual gift, or stop us from tending toward the fullness of love. The world could collapse around us, but it wouldn't rob us of the possibility of praying, placing all our trust in God, and loving.

That doesn't mean shutting ourselves in an ivory tower and being indifferent to what is going on around us, or remain passive. When there are problems, we should want them solved, and try to see what God is asking of us. Should we intervene? Can we do something positive? If the answer is yes, it would be a sin of omission to do nothing.

But if everything seems to be going wrong around us, it is all the more necessary to preserve our freedom to hope in God and serve him joyfully and enthusiastically. The devil often tries to discourage us and make us lose our joy in serving God. One means he uses particularly is to make us worry about everything that is not going well around us. Suppose, for example, we are living in community. To make us lose dynamism and spiritual energy, the devil will lead us to notice a host of negative things—the unfair attitudes of the people in charge, our brothers' and sisters' mistakes and lack of fervor, their faults (sometimes even serious ones), and so on. The weight of worry, insecurity, sadness, and discouragement will weaken our spiritual verve. What use it is to make such an effort to pray and be generous, when there are all these problems? It is a short step to lukewarmness. We must unmask this temptation and say: "No matter what happens, I've got nothing to lose. I need to maintain my fervor, continue to love God and pray with all my heart, and love the people I'm living with, even if I don't know how things will turn out. I won't be wasting my time, and it's not wrong to try to love. Love will never be in vain." St. John of the Cross said, "Where there is no love, put love, and you will harvest love." [56]

If problems cause us to become sad and lose our fervor, we've solved nothing, but only added another problem to the rest. If the sins of those around us lead us to become upset and discouraged, we are helping to spread the evil more rapidly. Evil is only overcome by good, and we can only put a stop to the spread of sin by fervor, joy, and hope, doing all the good we can today without worrying about tomorrow.

[56] St. John of the Cross, Letter 26, To Madre María de la Encarnación, discalced Carmelite in Segovia, July 6, 1591.

## *The real harm is not outside us but within us*

At times of struggle we need also to recall the conversion we should be concerned about is not our neighbor's but our own. Only if we take our own conversion seriously do we stand any chance of seeing our neighbor converted too. This point of view is realistic and encouraging. We have little real influence on other people, and our attempts to change them have only a very slight chance of success, since most of the time we want them to change in line with our criteria and aims more than God's. If we are concerned first with our own conversion, however, we have more hope of making a difference. It does more good to seek to reform our hearts than to reform the world or the Church. Everyone will benefit.

Let us ask ourselves this question: "To what degree can the evil in my surroundings affect me?" With apologies to those I am going to scandalize, I say that the evil around us—the sins of others, of people in the Church, of society—does not become an evil for us unless we let it penetrate our hearts.

The point isn't that we should become indifferent. Just the opposite. The holier we are, the more we will suffer due to the evil and sin in the world. But external evil only harms us to the degree we react badly to it, by fear, worry, discouragement, sadness, giving up, rushing to apply hasty solutions that don't solve anything, judging, fostering bitterness and resentment, refusing to forgive, and so on. Jesus says in St. Mark's Gospel: "There is nothing outside a man which by going into him can defile him; but the things which come out of a man are what defile him!" [57] Harm does not come to us from external circumstances, but from how we react to them interiorly. "What ruins our souls is not what happens outside, but the echo that it awakes within us." [58] *The harm that other people do to me never comes from them, it comes from me.* Harm is only self-inflicted, the Fathers of the Church said long ago.

## Our complicity increases the harm

When we concentrate too much on something that isn't right, and make it our main topic of conversation, we end up giving evil more substance than it has. Deploring evil sometimes only strengthens it. I recently heard a priest say, "I'm not going to spend my life denouncing sin. That would be doing it too much honor. I would rather encourage good than condemn evil." And I think he was right. This is not a head-in-the-sand attitude, but the optimism of charity. "Love is not irritable or resentful; it does not rejoice at wrong, but rejoices in the right. Love bears all things, believes all things, hopes all things, endures all things." [59]

[57] Mark 7: 14.

[58] Christiane Singer, *Du bon usage des crises* (On making good use of crises) (Paris: Albin Michel, 2001), p. 102.

[59] 1 Corinthians 13: 5–7.

As we ourselves advance more surely and effectively by giving ourselves totally to the good despite our defects, so also we do more to help others experience conversion and make progress by encouraging them in the positive aspects of their lives than by condemning their errors. Good is more real than evil, and it can overcome evil.

We sometimes experience a savage satisfaction in detecting and showing up something wrong. The resentment and bitterness we feel arise from a spiritual void within us and the sense of dissatisfaction it produces. Often, the most critical people are those with the greatest spiritual emptiness. One wonders whether they must create enemies for themselves in order to exist.

## *Evil comes to fill a gap*

Jesus was surrounded by a sea of evil, hatred, violence, and lies. His heart was broken and pierced, and he suffered more than anyone has ever suffered, but the wrong done to him did not penetrate him, because his heart was full of trust in his Father, abandonment, and loving self-offering. We "should follow in his steps . . . when he was reviled, he did not revile in return; when he suffered, he did not threaten." [60] So, too, with our Lady at the foot of the Cross. She drank the cup of suffering, but her heart remained pure. It held no fear, no rebellion, no

---

[60] 1 Peter 2:21, 23.

hatred, no despair, but only acceptance, forgiveness, and hope.

If the wrongs people commit do penetrate our hearts, that is because they find room there. If suffering makes us bitter and ill humored, it is because our hearts are devoid of faith, hope, and love. But if our hearts are filled with total trust in God and love for him and our neighbor, there is no room there for evil, hurt, and harm. St. Maximilian Kolbe died in the starvation bunker at Auschwitz, but his heart remained pure and intact in that hellish place, because he felt no hatred for his executioners and consented to give up his life for love. He and his companions sang the *Magnificat* as they were dying. They conquered evil with good.

The ability to remain untouched by evil is not acquired all at once. It is the fruit of a long process of self-conquest and grace that makes us grow in the theological virtues. It is an aspect of spiritual maturity, more a gift from God than the result of our efforts. But this gift will be given to us more quickly and surely, the more we strive for it, desire it, and try to practice the attitudes described here: rooting ourselves in God through faith and prayer; not blaming people and things around us for what isn't going well in our lives and stop seeing ourselves as victims; resolutely shouldering responsibilities and accepting our lives as they are; and using our present capacity for believing, hoping, and loving to the full at every moment.

## *The royal freedom of God's children*

In baptism we are anointed with sweet-smelling oil as the sign of our new character: by our union with Christ each of us is priest, prophet, and king. We are kings because we are children and heirs of the King of heaven and earth. But also in the sense that we are subject to nothing and everything is subject to us. This is what happens to us when we let the grace of baptism operate in us, living as God's children in faith, hope, and love. Yes, we know suffering and sorrow, but everything that happens serves to make us grow in love and in the fact of being God's children. What happens and how others behave can no longer touch us negatively; they can only promote our true good, which is to love.

St. Paul expresses that sense of royal freedom, the privilege of Christians living in the arms of God our Father, by saying: "All things are yours." And he adds: "And you are Christ's; and Christ is God's." [61] This also is beautifully expressed by St. John of the Cross in his "Prayer of the Soul in Love."

Why do you hesitate? Why do you wait? For you can from this instant love God in your heart. Mine are the heavens and mine is the earth, and mine are the peoples, the just are mine, and mine are the

[61] 1 Corinthians 3: 21, 23.

79

sinners; the angels are mine, and the Mother of God, and all things are mine, and God himself is mine and for me, because Christ is mine and wholly for me. What do you ask for, then, and what do you seek, my soul? All of that is yours, and for you.[62]

---

[62] St. John of the Cross, "Prayer of the Soul in Love," *Sayings of Light and Love.*

# II

## THE PRESENT MOMENT

### I. FREEDOM AND THE PRESENT MOMENT

One of the essential conditions of interior freedom is the ability to live in the present moment. For one thing, it is only then that we can exercise freedom. We have no hold on the past—we can't change the smallest bit of it. People sometimes try to relive past events considered failures ("I should have done this . . . I should have said that . . .") but those imaginary scenarios are merely dreams: it is not possible to backtrack. The only free act we can make in regard to the past is to accept it just as it was and leave it trustingly in God's hands.

We have very little hold on the future either. Despite all our foresight, plans, and promises, it takes very little to change everything completely. We can't program life in advance, but can only receive it moment by moment.

All we have is the present moment. Here is the only place where we can make free acts. Only in the present moment are we truly in contact with reality.

Someone might think it tragic that the present is so

fleeting and neither the past nor the future really belongs to us. But, approached from the standpoint of Christian faith and hope, the present moment is rich in grace and holds immense reassurance.

This is where God is present. "I am with you always, to the close of the age." [1] God is the eternal present. Every moment, whatever it brings, is filled with God's presence, rich with the possibility of communion with God. We do not commune with God in the past or the future, but by welcoming each instant as the place where he gives himself to us. We should learn to live in each moment as sufficient to itself for God is there; and if God is there, we lack nothing. We feel we are missing this or that, simply because we are living in the past or in the future instead of dwelling in each second. Psalm 145 says, "The eyes of all look to thee, and thou givest them their food in due season. Thou openest thy hand, thou satisfiest the desire of every living thing." [2]

There is something very liberating in this understanding of the grace of the present moment. Even if the whole of our past has been a disaster, even if our future seems like a dead end, *now* we can establish communion with God through an act of faith, trust, and abandonment. God is eternally present, eternally young, eternally new, and our past and future are his. He can forgive everything, purify everything, renew everything. "He will re-

[1] Matthew 28: 20.
[2] Psalm 145[144]: 15–16.

new you in his love." [3] In the present moment, because of his infinitely merciful love, we always have the possibility of starting again, not impeded by the past, or tormented by the future. The past is in the hands of the Merciful God, who can draw benefit from everything: the future is in the hands of the Providence of God who will never forget us. Faith keeps us from living as many people do, oppressed by a burdensome past and worrisome future. Living in the present permits our hearts to expand.

## 2. "TO LOVE" HAS A PRESENT TENSE ONLY

Treatises on spirituality speak of the stages of the spiritual life. They list three, seven, twelve, or whatever number the particular author prefers. There is much to be learned from these accounts, whether it is the seven mansions of the soul depicted by St. Teresa of Avila or the twelve degrees of humility of the Rule of St. Benedict.

But experience has taught me a different approach. I often say jokingly that the ladder of perfection has only one step: the step we take *today*. Without concerning ourselves about the past or the future, we can decide to believe today, place all our trust in God today, love God and neighbor today. Whether our good resolutions produce success or failure, next day we can begin again, not relying on our strength but only on God's faithfulness.

This attitude is fundamental in the spiritual life. St.

[3] Zephaniah 3: 17.

Paul describes it: "Forgetting what lies behind and straining forward to what lies ahead, I press on toward the goal for the prize of the upward call of God in Christ Jesus. . . . Only let us hold true to what we have attained." [4] It is a basic note of monastic spirituality. St. Anthony of Egypt (the Father of Monasticism, who died at the age of 105 and who, when he was 100, used to say, "I haven't yet begun to be converted!") would repeat St. Paul's words unceasingly. His biographer, St. Athanasius, adds: "He also remembered the words of Elijah: 'The Lord liveth before whom I stand today.' St. Anthony pointed out that when Elijah said 'today' he took no account of the past. And so, as though he were still at the beginning, every day he strove to live as he wished to appear before God: pure of heart and ready to obey God's will and no other." [5] The same attitude has been practiced by all the saints, St. Thérèse of Lisieux being a shining example. She wrote: "To love thee, O Jesus, I have but today." [6]

### 3. WE CAN SUFFER FOR ONLY ONE MOMENT

This effort to live in the reality of each moment is of the greatest importance in times of suffering. St. Thérèse of Lisieux said during her illness: "I only suffer for one moment. It is because people think about the past and the

[4] Philippians 3: 13–16.
[5] St. Athanasius of Alexandria, *Life of St. Anthony*, chapter 2.
[6] St. Thérèse of Lisieux, *Poésie* PN5.

future that they become discouraged and despair."[7] Nobody has the capacity to suffer for ten or twenty years; but we have the grace to bear today the suffering that is ours now. Projecting things into the future crushes us—not experiencing suffering but anticipating it.

> . . . Reality is something one shoulders together with all the suffering that goes with it. . . . But the idea of suffering (which is not the reality, for real suffering is always fruitful and can turn life into a precious thing) must be destroyed. And if you destroy the ideas behind which life lies imprisoned as behind bars, then you liberate your true life, its real mainsprings, and you will also have the strength to bear real suffering, your own and the world's.[8]

## 4. "LET THE DAY'S OWN TROUBLE BE SUFFICIENT FOR THE DAY"

One of the wisest sayings in the Gospel is "Let the day's own trouble be sufficient for the day."[9] Let us absorb this lesson Jesus teaches. We often complain about how much we are suffering, without realizing that it's our fault. As if today's suffering weren't enough, we add regrets about the past and worries for the future! It's no surprise we feel

[7] St. Thérèse of Lisieux, "Yellow Notebook," August 19.

[8] Hillesum, *Interrupted Life*, p. 269.

[9] Matthew 6: 34.

overwhelmed. For life to be bearable, we must practice bearing today's problems only.

The past casts its shadow over the present whenever we brood about old failures and yesterday's choices. Of course we should ask God's forgiveness for our faults and should learn from them where appropriate. But once we've said we're sorry and meant it, that is enough. While seeking to make amends where possible for the harm we have caused, most of the time we should simply leave things in God's hands, trusting him to put everything right. We must put a stop to attitudes or thoughts that keep us from living trustingly in the present moment.

Sometimes we feel we've wasted much time and missed all too many opportunities to love and grow. If the feeling leads to real repentance and to starting again courageously and trustingly, then it is something positive. But if the sense of time wasted gets us down and makes us feel we have ruined our lives, we must reject it. To lock ourselves in the past would only add another sin to those already committed. It would be a serious lack of trust in the infinite mercy and power of God, who loves us and wants always to offer us a new chance to become holy, despite the past. When the thought of how little progress we've made threatens to overwhelm us, we must make an act of faith and hope, such as: "Thank you, my God, for *all* my past. I firmly believe that you can draw good out of everything I have lived through. I want to have no regrets, and I resolve today to begin from zero, with exactly the same trust as if all my past history were made up of nothing but faithfulness and holiness." Nothing could please God more than that!

### 5. TOMORROW CAN TAKE CARE OF ITSELF

If it's a mistake to add the burden of the past to the weight of the present, it's a still worse mistake to burden the present with the future. The remedy for that tendency is to meditate on the lesson contained in the Gospel about abandonment to God's Providence and ask for God's grace to practice it. "Do not be anxious about your life, what you shall eat or what you shall drink, nor about your body, what you shall put on. Is not life more than food, and the body more than clothing? Look at the birds of the air; they neither sow nor reap nor gather into barns, and yet your heavenly Father feeds them. Are you not of more value than they? And which of you by being anxious can add one cubit to his span of life? . . . Therefore do not be anxious, saying 'What shall we eat?' or 'What shall we drink?' or 'What shall we wear?' " [10]

Again, this does not mean being improvident and irresponsible. We are obliged to plan for the future and take thought for tomorrow. But we should do it *without worrying*, without the care that gnaws at the heart but doesn't solve anything—and often prevents us from putting our hearts into what we have to do here and now. Hearts

[10] Matthew 6: 25–34.

anxious about tomorrow can't be open to the grace of the present moment.

Like the manna that fed the Hebrew people in the desert, grace can't be stockpiled. We can't build up reserves of grace but only receive it moment by moment, as part of the "daily bread" we pray for in the Our Father. To be free of the burden of the future as well as the past, we need "re-education." Here are some commonsense points that can help.

Things seldom happen as we expect. Most of our fears and apprehensions turn out to be completely imaginary. Difficulties we anticipated become very simple in reality; and the real difficulties are things that didn't occur to us. It's better to accept things as they come, one after another, trusting that we will have the grace to deal with them at the right time, than to invent a host of scenarios about what may happen—scenarios that normally turn out to be wrong. The best way to prepare for the future is to put our hearts into the present. In the Gospel, Jesus tells his disciples they will be hauled before tribunals, and then he adds: "Settle it therefore in your minds, not to meditate beforehand how to answer; for I will give you a mouth and wisdom, which none of your adversaries will be able to withstand or contradict." [11]

Projecting our fears into the future cuts us off from reality and prevents us from dealing with the present

[11] Luke 21: 14–15.

situation as we should. It saps our best energies. In another passage of her journal, Etty Hillesum says: "If one burdens the future with one's worries, it cannot grow organically. I am filled with confidence, not that I shall succeed in worldly things, but that even when things go badly for me I shall still find life good and worth living." [12]

Fear of suffering, as we've seen, causes more pain than suffering does. We need to live accordingly.

> We have to fight them daily, like fleas, those many small worries about the morrow, for they sap our energies. We make mental provision for the days to come, and everything turns out differently, quite differently. Sufficient unto the day. The things that have to be done must be done, and for the rest we must not allow ourselves to become infested with thousands of petty fears and worries, so many motions of no confidence in God. Everything will turn out all right. . . . Ultimately, we have just one moral duty: to reclaim large areas of peace in ourselves, more and more peace, and to reflect it towards others. And the more peace there is in us, the more peace there will also be in our troubled world. [13]

[12] Hillesum, *Interrupted Life*, pp. 212–213.
[13] Ibid., pp. 266–267.

## 6. LIVE, INSTEAD OF WAITING TO LIVE

Our present life is always something good, for the Creator has endowed it with a blessing he will never cancel, even though sin has complicated things. "God saw that it was good," the Book of Genesis tells us. For God, "seeing" means not merely taking note but actually conferring reality. This fundamental goodness of life is also expressed by Jesus: "Is not life more than food, and the body more than clothing?" [14]

Sometimes, though, it isn't worry that causes us to focus on the future, but the hope of something better or happier. It may be a very specific event, like a reunion with someone we love or coming home after a long, tiring journey. Or it may be less well-defined: the time when things will go better, circumstances will change, life will be more interesting. At present, we tell ourselves, we don't really have a life, but later we will "live life to the full." There is nothing wrong with that, but it does contain a certain danger. We may spend our whole lives *waiting to live*. Thus we risk not fully accepting the reality of our present lives. Yet, what guarantee is there that we won't be disappointed when the long-awaited time arrives? Meanwhile we don't put our hearts sufficiently into today, and so miss graces we should be receiving. Let us live each moment to the full, not worrying about whether time is

[14] Matthew 6: 25.

going quickly or slowly but welcoming everything given us moment by moment.

To live today well we also should remember that God only asks for one thing at a time, never two. It doesn't matter whether the job we have in hand is sweeping the kitchen floor or giving a speech to forty thousand people. We must to put our hearts into it, simply and calmly, and not try to solve more than one problem at a time. Even when what we're doing is genuinely trifling, it's a mistake to rush through it as though we felt we were wasting our time. If something, no matter how ordinary, needs to be done and is part of our lives, it's worth doing for its own sake, and worth putting our hearts into.

### 7. AVAILABILITY TO OTHER PEOPLE

Availability is fundamental in our relations with others. In every encounter with someone else, however long or short, we should make him feel we're one hundred percent there for him at that moment, with nothing else to do except be with him and do whatever needs doing for him. Good manners, yes, but also real, heartfelt availability. This is very difficult, since we have a strong sense of proprietary rights to our time and easily tend to get upset if we can't organize it as we choose. But this is the price of genuine love. If Jesus asks us not to have any worries, that is mainly to safeguard the quality of our relations with other people. A heart preoccupied by concerns and worries isn't available to other people. Parents should remember this: children can get along happily without constantly demanding their parents' attention, provided there are regular times when Dad or Mom have no concern except being with them. If we are riddled with anxieties instead of leaving them in God's hands, we can't offer our children that kind of time, and they will never feel secure in our love, no matter how many expensive gifts we lavish on them.

### 8. PSYCHOLOGICAL TIME AND INTERIOR TIME

If we try to live like that and deepen our relationship with God and our prayer life, so that we can perceive his presence within us and live as much as possible in communion with his indwelling, we shall discover something wonderful: the interior rhythm of grace that our life follows at its deepest level.

It might be said that there are two modes of time: time of the head and time of the heart. The first is psychological time, the time in our minds, which we make calculations about, and divide into hours and days to be managed and planned. This kind of time always goes either too fast or too slowly.

But there is another sort of time, experienced at certain moments of happiness or grace, though it always exists. This is God's time, the time of the deep rhythms of grace in our lives. It is composed of a succession of moments harmoniously linked. Each of those moments is complete in itself, full, because in it we do what we have to do, in communion with God's will. That time is communion with eternity. It is time we receive as a gift.

If we always lived in that time, we would have much less opportunity for harm and wrongdoing. The devil slips into time we live badly because we are refusing something or grasping too eagerly at something else.

The saints habitually lived in that interior time. To do that required great inner freedom, total detachment from our own plans and programs and inclinations. We must be ready to do in an instant just what we hadn't expected, to live in total self-abandonment, with no other concern than doing God's will and being fully available to people and events. We also need to experience in prayer God's presence within us and to listen inwardly to the Holy Spirit so as to follow his suggestions.

Then nothing is left to chance. Often we may journey in darkness, but we sense that our lives are unfolding in a rhythm we do not control but to which we are happy to abandon ourselves and by which all events are arranged with infinite wisdom.

# III

## THE DYNAMISM OF
## FAITH, HOPE, AND LOVE

### I. THE THEOLOGICAL VIRTUES

The importance of faith, hope, and love has come up frequently in the preceding chapters. They are classically termed "theological virtues," in other words, the virtues that connect us to God. We can only acquire interior freedom to the degree we develop these three virtues.

Today, "virtue" has lost much of its meaning. Its derivation is the Latin word *virtus*, meaning strength or power. The theological virtue of faith is strength for us. The Letter to the Romans says of Abraham: "No distrust made him waver concerning the promise of God, but he grew strong in his faith as he gave glory to God, fully convinced that God was able to do what he had promised." [1] Hope, likewise, is not vague and dreamy, but confidence in the faithfulness of God who will fulfill his promises—confidence that gives us great strength. And

[1] Romans 4: 20.

theological charity could be called the courage to love God and neighbor.

These three theological virtues constitute the essential dynamic of Christian life. It is crucial to understand their role and center our whole spiritual life on them rather than, as sometimes happens, on secondary aspects. For Christians, maturity means the ability to live by faith, hope, and love. Christians are not people who follow a set of rules. Christians are, first and foremost, people who believe in God, hope for everything from him, and want to love him with all their hearts and to love their neighbors. The commandments, prayer, the sacraments, and all the graces that come from God (including the loftiest mystical experiences) have just one purpose: to increase our faith, hope, and love.

The New Testament, especially in the Letters of St. Paul, depicts faith, hope, and love at the heart of Christian life. "We give thanks to God . . . remembering before our God and Father your work of faith and labor of love and steadfastness of hope in our Lord Jesus Christ." [2] In the spiritual combat, a Christian's weapons are essentially the theological virtues: "Let us . . . put on the breastplate of faith and love, and for a helmet, the hope of salvation." [3]

The theological virtues have a key role in the spiritual life because here our freedom and God's grace cooperate. Everything in our lives that is positive and good comes

[2] 1 Thessalonians 1: 2–3.
[3] 1 Thessalonians 5: 8.

from God's grace, the unmerited and freely given action of the Holy Spirit in our hearts; yet grace cannot be fully fruitful in us unless we fully cooperate. "I have created you without you, but I will not save you without you," said our Lord to St. Catherine of Siena.

The theological virtues, then, are mysteriously but really God's gift and our action. Faith is a free gift from God: no one can say "Jesus is Lord" unless it is granted to him by the Holy Spirit. But it is at the same time a person's act of voluntary consent to the truth proposed by Scripture and the Tradition of the Church. Its voluntary side is most clear in times of temptation or doubt: "I believe what I want to believe," said St. Thérèse of Lisieux amid the trials she endured at the end of her life. Believing does not always come naturally, and it sometimes requires us to take our courage in both hands to put an end to hesitation and doubt. Still, when we make an act of faith, it is only possible because "the Holy Spirit helps us in our weakness." [4]

In the same way hope is a choice that often demands an effort. It is easier to worry, get discouraged, be afraid. Hoping means *trusting*. When we hope we are not passive: we are acting.

Love is also a decision. Sometimes it comes spontaneously, but very often loving people will mean choosing to love them. Otherwise love would be no more than emo-

[4] Romans 8: 26.

96

tion, even selfishness, and not something that engages our freedom.

But always it is through an act of God, hidden or open, that faith, hope, and charity are possible.[5] The theological virtues awaken and grow in human hearts by the work and teaching of the Holy Spirit. That divine teaching is sometimes quite disconcerting. Let us look at the way the Holy Spirit acts within us.

## 2. THE THREE OUTPOURINGS OF THE HOLY SPIRIT

There is no way to chart all the Spirit does in any life. We can't set rules for it or plan it. "The wind blows where it wills, and you hear the sound of it, but you do not know whence it comes or whither it goes."[6] Yet, certain constants can be traced. The mysteries of the Rosary can help us see that.

The Rosary is a very beautiful prayer through which we entrust ourselves to our Lady in order to enter into communion with the events of Christ's life. But it is also a kind of symbol of every human life. Just as the Rosary contains joyful, sorrowful, and finally glorious mysteries,

[5] There is a difficult question here. How can a human act (the act of believing, hoping, or loving) be a fully human, free and voluntary act, and at the same time a gift from God, the fruit of the Holy Spirit's action in a person's heart? This touches on the deep mystery of the "interaction" between God's acts and our freedom; suffer here to say there is no contradiction between God's actions and human freedom: God is the creator of our freedom, and the more God influences our hearts, the freer he makes us. The acts we make under the influence of the Holy Spirit come from God, but they are also fully free, fully voluntary, fully our own.

[6] John 3: 8.

it could be said of the work of the Holy Spirit in our lives that there are "outpourings" that are joyful, sorrowful, and glorious. (That is the order of their importance, but they occur in a cyclical way.)

Some outpourings of the Holy Spirit illuminate and reveal, some strip and impoverish, and some confirm and fortify. All three kinds are necessary: the first to give birth to faith, the second to teach us hope, and the third to give us the courage to love.

Let's take the example of the life of St. Peter. I sometimes ask people of the Charismatic Renewal: "When did St. Peter receive the outpouring of the Holy Spirit?" They usually answer: "At Pentecost!" This is true of course, but I add that that was not the only time. In my opinion, Peter experienced other "outpourings of the Holy Spirit" before the one in Acts. There are at least two I love to recall.

### 3. VOCATION AND THE GIFT OF FAITH

The first outpouring of the Holy Spirit in St. Peter's life occurred at the moment of his vocation, when he felt impelled to leave everything—job, nets, boat, and family—to follow Jesus. Peter was profoundly moved by Jesus' message, and above all by Jesus himself. "No man ever spoke like this man!" [7] He was seized with enthusiasm for the prophet from Galilee, sensing that his words were

[7] John 7: 46.

words of eternal life. At the same time he guessed that, by responding to Jesus' call, "Come, follow me," his life was destined to take a completely new turn and would be dedicated from then on to an extraordinary venture. The Holy Spirit revealed to Peter both who Jesus was and the new meaning of his own existence, arousing great joy and happiness in him. It was the beginning of a wonderful spiritual adventure.

These were "joyful outpourings" of the Holy Spirit. The Spirit enriches us, too, with a new presence of Christ and a new understanding of the meaning of our lives. At such times the Spirit's main role is to enlighten us and awaken a response of *faith*.

### 4. ST. PETER'S TEARS, AND THE GIFT OF HOPE

But the Holy Spirit sometimes impoverishes us. Peter's supreme experience of this kind was at the most terrible point in his life: his denial of Jesus. But through God's mercy that denial became the occasion of a deep outpouring of the Holy Spirit. The Prince of the Apostles wept for his own baseness and sin, but in his tears he received the hope of forgiveness.

Peter's denial of his Lord was a terrible fall for him. He was the head of the Apostles. Jesus had chosen him for that. But all his noble sentiments and keen sense of responsibility toward the other disciples crumbled in just a few seconds. All it took was a servant girl in the High Priest's courtyard who asked: "Are not you also one of this man's disciples?"[8] Three times Peter denied his Master, swearing he had nothing to do with him. But the Holy Spirit, Father of the poor, made use of this terrible fall to touch the Apostle's heart again, very deeply. Peter met Jesus' eyes and understood the full horror of his betrayal. But at the same time he saw that he was not being condemned but loved more tenderly than ever. For him there was still the hope of being lifted up again, the hope of salvation. And Peter broke down in tears, in which his heart was purified there and then. Judas, why did you avoid Jesus' eyes, and so trap yourself in your own despair? Right up until the very end the hope of salvation and forgiveness could have been yours. Your sin was no worse than Peter's. . . .

In Jesus' gaze Peter received an outpouring of the Holy Spirit. One of those sorrowful outpourings that impoverish us but ultimately are infinitely profitable because they show us our powerlessness and oblige us from then on to trust exclusively in God's mercy and faithfulness.

"Someone who sees his own sin is greater than someone who raises the dead," the Desert Fathers said. Peter passed from presumption to *hope*. Hope is the virtue of people who know they are infinitely weak and easily broken, and rely firmly on God with utter trust. Peter for the first time in his life made a real *act of hope*: "What I'm not capable of doing by my own strength, I hope for from

[8] John 18: 17.

you, O my God. Not by virtue of my merits, because I have none, but by virtue of your mercy alone."

Theological hope can only come from a radical experience of our poverty. As long as we are rich, we rely on our riches. To learn hope, we have to pass through impoverishment. These experiences are the prelude to experiencing the goodness, faithfulness, and power of God in a quite extraordinary way. "Blessed are the poor in spirit"—those stripped of everything by the Spirit—"for theirs is the kingdom of heaven." [9]

### 5. PENTECOST AND THE GIFT OF CHARITY

Turning to the glorious mysteries, we find that Pentecost was clearly a "glorious outpouring" of the Holy Spirit for Peter and the other disciples. It filled them—and fills us—with God's presence and united them closely to Christ; its most beautiful fruit is the *courage to love*. In the Cenacle, Peter received power from on high as Jesus had promised. [10] This was the power of charity, the fire of love, the courage to love God more than anyone or anything else and to consecrate his life to serving his neighbor through preaching the Gospel. Burning with the charity poured out in his heart by the Holy Spirit, Peter from then on was a tireless Apostle, rejoicing in his opportunities to suffer for the name of Jesus, [11] and

[9] Matthew 5: 3.
[10] Luke 24: 40; Acts 1: 8.
[11] Acts 5: 41.

totally dedicated to "tending the flock of God that was in his charge willingly." [12]

## 6. THE FIRE THAT LIGHTS UP, BURNS, AND TRANSFIGURES

These three aspects of the spiritual life—the joyful, sorrowful, and glorious outpourings of the Holy Spirit—recall the image of the fire and the log used by St. John of the Cross. [13]

When fire approaches the log it first lights it up and warms it. That corresponds to a joyful mystery. We are warmed by the love of God revealed to us. When the fire comes closer, the wood begins to blacken, smoke, smell bad, and give out tar and other unpleasant substances. This is the sorrowful outpouring: the soul has the painful experience of its own wretchedness. This phase lasts until the purifying fire has completed its work and the soul is totally transformed into a fire of love. Here is the glorious outpouring, in which the soul is strengthened in charity, the fire Jesus came to kindle on earth.

The lesson of this imagery is very optimistic: we should not fear the times when we feel crushed by our wretchedness. We should abandon ourselves trustingly to God, sure that sooner or later wretchedness will be transformed into burning charity. St. Thérèse of Lisieux wrote to her

---

[12] Compare his exhortation to the elders of the Church in his Epistle: 1 Peter 5: 2–3.

[13] St. John of the Cross, *The Dark Night of the Soul*, book 2, chap. 19.

sister, Marie du Sacré-Coeur: "Let us keep far from everything that shines, let's love our littleness . . . then we will be poor in spirit, and Jesus will come and look for us. However far away we are, he will transform us into flames of love." [14]

### 7. THE DYNAMISM OF THE THEOLOGICAL VIRTUES

St. Seraphim of Sarov said the aim of Christian life is the acquisition of the Holy Spirit. To that one could add— and the events of the life of St. Peter demonstrate this— that the Holy Spirit's aim in our life is to awaken the theological virtues of faith, hope, and charity in us and make them grow. All the other charisms, gifts, or operations of grace are only means he uses to increase faith, hope, and love.

The three theological virtues cannot be separated. None can really exist without the other two. The most important is obviously charity, or love. "At the evening of our lives, we will be judged on love," said St. John of the Cross. We should re-read the wonderful hymn to charity in the First Letter to the Corinthians: "If I have all faith, so as to remove mountains, but have not love, I am nothing." [15] Later St. Paul adds: "So faith, hope, love abide, these three; but the greatest of these is love." [16] Faith and hope are provisional; they exist only for this earth and will

[14] Letter 197, September 17, 1896.
[15] 1 Corinthians 13: 2.
[16] 1 Corinthians 13: 13.

pass away. In heaven, faith will be replaced by sight, and hope by possession; only love will never pass away. It will never be replaced by anything else, because it is the goal of all. On this earth, love is the fullest participation in the life of heaven, and faith and hope exist for its sake.

But love cannot exist without its two "servants," faith and hope. It needs them to be able to grow and develop. Next we shall see why.

### 8. LOVE NEEDS HOPE; HOPE IS BASED ON FAITH

There can be no charity without hope. Love needs space to grow and flourish; it is a marvelous thing, but in a sense fragile. The special "environment" it needs is made up of hope. If love does not grow or turns cold, very often that's because it is stifled by cares, fears, worries, or discouragements. Jesus told St. Faustina: "The greatest obstacles to holiness are discouragement and worry." [17]

We were created to love. Whether we are or aren't aware of it, one of our deepest aspirations is to give ourselves to another. A Gospel parable represents love as growing in our hearts like wheat that, having been sown, sprouts and grows by itself, whether the farmer watches or sleeps.[18] Yet love often fails to grow. Its development is blocked by selfishness, pride, "the cares of the world and the delight in riches," [19] as Jesus says, or other bar-

---

[17] St. Faustina, *Petit journal*, p. 480.
[18] Mark 4: 26.
[19] Matthew 13: 22.

riers. Most often, the root of the problem is a lack of hope.

Lacking hope, we don't really believe God can make us happy, and so we construct our happiness out of covetousness and lust. We don't wait to find the fullness of our existence in God, and so we shape an artificial identity grounded in pride. Or else—the most common condition among people of good will—we would like to love and be generous in loving and giving ourselves, but we are held back by fears, hesitations, and worries. Lack of trust in what God's grace can do in our lives, and what we can do with his help, leads to a shrinkage of the heart, a lessening of charity. But, as St. Thérèse of Lisieux said, trust leads to love.

When we lose fervor, zest, generosity in loving God and neighbor, it is very often because of discouragement or even a sort of secret despair. The remedy is to *rekindle our hope*, to rediscover a new trust in what God can do for us (no matter how weak and wretched we are) and what we can accomplish with the help of his grace.

"Discouragement is what ruins souls," the Venerable Francis Mary Paul Libermann used to say. So the best treatment is to discover the root of discouragement and learn again to look at that particular aspect of one's life with eyes of hope.

For the will to be strong and enterprising, it needs to be animated by desire. Desire can only be strong if what is desired is perceived as accessible, possible. We cannot effectively want something if we have the sense that "we'll never make it." When the will is weak, we must re-present the object so that it again is seen as accessible. Hope is the virtue that effects. Through hope, we know we can confidently expect everything from God. "I can do all things in him who strengthens me," [20] says St. Paul. Hope enables love to expand and thrive.

But for hope to be a real force in our lives, it needs a solid foundation, a bedrock of truth. That solid foundation is given by faith: we can "hope against hope" [21] because we "know whom we have believed." [22] Faith makes us cling firmly to the truth handed on by Scripture, which tells of the goodness of God, his mercy, and his absolute faithfulness to his promises. The Epistle to the Hebrews says: "We who have fled for refuge might have strong encouragement to seize the hope set before us. We have this as a sure and steadfast anchor of the soul, a hope that enters into the inner shrine behind the curtain, where Jesus has gone as a forerunner on our behalf." [23]

Scripture reveals the absolutely unconditional and irrevocable love of God for his children, shown in Christ who was born and died and rose again for us. He "loved me, and gave himself for me." [24] Through faith our hearts

[20] Philippians 4: 13.
[21] See Romans 4: 18.
[22] See 2 Timothy 1: 12.
[23] Hebrews 6: 18–20.
[24] Galatians 2: 20.

hold on to that truth and find in it immense and indestructible hope. "Faith is the mother of love and hope, as
well as trust and confidence." [25]

## 9. THE KEY ROLE OF HOPE

These considerations show the key role of hope in Christian life. It could be said that, while charity is the greatest
of the three theological virtues, in practice hope is the
most important. As long as hope remains, love develops.
If hope is extinguished, love grows cold. A world without
hope soon becomes a world without love. But hope needs
faith, from which it springs. St. John Climacus, a seventh-
century Father of the Church, says "faith brings what
seemed hopeless within our reach." He adds: "A man of
faith is not one who believes that God can do everything,
but one who believes he can obtain everything from
God."

Let us meditate on these words of St. John of the Cross,
which were decisive in encouraging Thérèse of Lisieux on
her "little way of trust and love": "We obtain from God as
much as we hope for from him." [26] God does not give
according to our merits, but according to our hope.

But hope can only be born in poverty. That is why
poverty of spirit is the key to all real growth in love.

[25] Catherine de Hueck Doherty, *Poustinia: Christian Spirituality of the East for Western Man* (Notre Dame, Ind.: Ave Maria Press, 1975); revised edition with new subtitle: *Poustinia: Encountering God in Silence, Solitude, and Prayer* (Comber-mere, Ont.: Madonna House, 2000).

[26] St. John of the Cross, *The Dark Night of the Soul*, book 2, chap. 10.

"Blessed are the poor in spirit, for theirs is the Kingdom of Heaven." [27]

### 10. DYNAMISM OF SIN, DYNAMISM OF GRACE

Faith, then, produces hope, and hope makes love possible and helps it grow. This dynamism of the theological virtues is the fruit of grace, the work of the Holy Spirit, but it passes through the cooperation of our will. This positive dynamism is opposed, point by point, to the negative dynamism of sin:

| faith | $\rightarrow$ | hope | $\rightarrow$ | love |
|-------|---------------|----------|---------------|------|
| doubt | $\rightarrow$ | distrust | $\rightarrow$ | sin |

How sin takes possession of the heart can be seen in the story of the fall of Adam and Eve in the second chapter of Genesis. At the root of sin lies *doubt*, suspicion of God. Is God really as good as he says? Can one trust his word? Is he really Father? Doubt gives rise to *distrust*: we don't believe God can fulfill us and make us happy. Then we try to manage on our own, in disobedience. This is the birth of selfishness, covetousness, lust, jealousy, fear, conflict, violence, and the whole network of evil.

Faith is the root of our cure and our liberation, the start of a life-giving process that heals the death engendered by sin. This is why Jesus lays such stress on faith. "If you have faith as a grain of mustard seed, you will say to this

---

[27] Matthew 5: 3.

mountain, 'Move hence to yonder place,' and it will move." [28] "Faith is the assurance of things hoped for," [29] says the Letter to the Hebrews.

### 11. HOPE AND PURITY OF HEART

This in turn highlights the key role of hope, which enables love to grow and flourish. The essence of Christian spiritual combat is, with the strength of faith, to maintain a hopeful outlook on every situation, on ourselves, on other people, on the Church and the world. Such an outlook enables us to react to every situation by loving.

The beatitude "Blessed are the pure in heart, for they shall see God" [30] contains one of the Gospel's most beautiful promises. St. John makes a striking connection between hope and purity of heart. "See what love the Father has given us, that we should be called children of God; and so we are. The reason why the world does not know us is that it did not know him. Beloved, we are God's children now; it does not yet appear what we shall be, but we know that when he appears we shall be like him, for we shall see him as he is." And the Apostle continues: "And everyone who thus hopes in him purifies himself as he is pure." [31]

This astonishing statement is perfectly in line with the

[28] Matthew 17: 20.
[29] Hebrews 11: 1.
[30] Matthew 5: 8.
[31] 1 John 3: 1–3.

great prophetic tradition of the Old Testament, where pure-hearted people are not so much those free of all faults and all wounds, as those who put all their hope in God and are certain his promises will be fulfilled. The pure-hearted expect everything from God; they hope in him and *in him alone.* Impurity of heart is duplicity the prophets denounced so often: that of people who, lacking complete trust in God, pray to idols, shopping around for salvation.

The pure of heart shall see God in eternity. But even now, in this life, they will be able to see God acting. God will respond to the hope they place in him, and will intervene in their favor.

The greatest poet of hope is Charles Péguy. In *The Portal of the Mystery of Hope,*[32] God says:

If it were from limpid days that she made limpid days.
If it were with souls, with clear water that she made her
    springs.
From clear water that she made clear water.
If it were from pure souls that she made pure souls,
Heavens, that would be nothing. Anyone could do as much.
    And there wouldn't be any secret to it.

But it's from sullied water, old water, stale water.
But it's from an impure soul that she makes a pure soul and
    that's the most beautiful secret in the whole garden of
    the world.

---

[32] Charles Péguy, *The Portal of the Mystery of Hope*, trans. D. L. Schindler (Grand Rapids, Mich.: Eerdmans; Edinburgh: T & T Clark, 1996), pp. 107–109.

# IV

## FROM LAW TO GRACE:
## LOVE AS A FREE GIFT

### I. LAW AND GRACE

St. Paul often speaks about Christian freedom. He is an ardent defender of the "glorious liberty of the children of God." [1]

Thus in the Letter to the Galatians we read: "For freedom Christ has set us free; stand fast therefore, and do not submit again to a yoke of slavery." [2] Paul is very concerned lest believers lose the precious freedom won for them by Christ. "I am astonished that you are so quickly deserting him who called you in the grace of Christ, and turning to a different Gospel." [3] "O foolish Galatians! Who has bewitched you, before whose eyes Jesus Christ was publicly portrayed as crucified?" [4]

But how are Christians threatened with losing their

[1] Romans 8:21.
[2] Galatians 5:1.
[3] Galatians 1:6.
[4] Galatians 3:1.

freedom? In chapter 5, the Apostle denounces the two "traps" that can cause this loss: the *law* and the *flesh*.

## 2. "WHERE THE SPIRIT RULES, THERE IS FREEDOM."
### THE DIFFERENCE BETWEEN FREEDOM
### AND LICENTIOUSNESS

The trap of the flesh[5] is discussed in verses 13–25. It is easy to understand. Instead of following the impulses of the Spirit, people give themselves up, under a pretext of freedom, to their passions, to selfishness, and sin in all its forms: "immorality, impurity, licentiousness, idolatry, sorcery, enmity, strife, jealousy, anger, selfishness, dissention, party spirit, envy, drunkenness, carousing and the like." St. Paul reminds us of a classic teaching worth repeating in these confused times: licentiousness is not freedom. It is slavery, in which people are trapped by what is most superficial in humanity: selfish desires, fears, weaknesses, and so on. We must wage an unceasing fight against the tendencies described by St. Paul and must remain permanently open to the healing graces that come from the Cross of Christ. Then we become truly capable of accomplishing good.

The basic theme underlying St. Paul's teaching is rejection of idolatry. Those who want to be faithful to the Lord are invited to guard their freedom and not give

[5] "Flesh" here does not mean the body, but human nature as wounded and sinful: that in man which resists God.

themselves up to worshiping idols: in other words, not look to things of this world—pleasures of the senses, power, fame, work, or a particular relationship—for the fullness, peace, happiness, and security that God alone can give. Otherwise we will be prey to bitter disappointment and will harm ourselves and other people seriously.

For today's reader, it is necessary to add that there are two things to be aware of if the fight against evil inclinations is to have any chance of success. First, our efforts will never be sufficient on their own. Only the grace of Christ can win us the victory. Therefore our chief weapons are prayer, patience, and hope. Second, one passion can only be cured by another—a misplaced love by a greater love, wrong behavior by right behavior that makes provisions for the desire underlying the wrongdoing, recognizes the conscious or unconscious needs that seek fulfillment and either offers them legitimate satisfaction or transfers them to something compatible with the person's calling.

### 3. THE TRAP OF THE LAW

St. Paul wants us to understand that there is another trap for Christian freedom that is more subtle, harder to see, and therefore perhaps ultimately more dangerous: the trap of the law. This is another manifestation of the "flesh," though not expressed in immoral behavior (it can appear to be the strictest morality). It replaces the rule of *grace* with the rule of *law*. This is a perversion of the Gospel.

The historical circumstances that impelled St. Paul to write about this topic are well known. After he had preached the Gospel, others "corrected" his teaching by telling his recent Christian converts they couldn't be saved without accepting circumcision and obeying the many prescriptions of the law of Moses. St. Paul reacted energetically, telling them that in following this counsel they would be "severed from Christ . . . fallen away from grace." [6] The law in itself is good, but the trap is this: if we take obeying the law as a condition for salvation, we are saying salvation comes, not from God's freely given love, but from our own deeds. The two modes of thought are directly opposed to each other. According to grace, we receive salvation and the love of God freely through Christ, quite apart from our merits, and freely respond to that love by the good works the Holy Spirit enables us to accomplish. According to the law, we merit salvation and the love of God by our good works. One approach is based on God's free, unconditional love, and the other on our capacities and ourselves.

St. Paul is deeply convinced that the salvation received in Christ is free and undeserved. He often underlines this, as in his letter to Titus: "For we ourselves were once foolish, disobedient, led astray, slaves to various passions and pleasures, passing our days in malice and envy, hated by men and hating one another; but when the goodness

6 Galatians 5: 4.

and loving kindness of God our Savior appeared, he saved us, not because of deeds done by us in righteousness, but in virtue of his own mercy, by the washing of regeneration and renewal in the Holy Spirit." [7] He writes the Ephesians: "God, who is rich in mercy, out of the great love with which he loved us, even when we were dead through our trespasses, made us alive together with Christ (by grace you have been saved), and raised us up with him, and made us sit with him in the heavenly places in Christ Jesus." [8]

What the law tells us to do is good. But taking law as the foundation for our relationship to God contradicts the truth that salvation is given freely and ends up killing love.

It can lead to pride. We may think we can fulfill all that the law prescribes, consider ourselves righteous, and despise other people for not doing the same. That was the sin of the Pharisees, which Jesus denounced so forcefully. Nothing more effectively kills love and compassion toward neighbor. But the law can also lead to despair, to the feeling that if we can't perfectly fulfill all its ordinances, we are irretrievably damned. It is certain that people who start by priding themselves on their spiritual "successes" will fall into despair sooner or later.

The process has variations. One is the rigid devotion of people who in everything act out of duty, as though they had a debt to pay to God. In reality, Christ has paid all

[7] Titus 3: 3–4. See also 2 Timothy 1: 9.
[8] Ephesians 2: 4–6.

mankind's debts to God on the Cross; he calls us to give him everything in return out of love and gratitude, not as repayment of a debt. There are people motivated by fear, always guilty and unable to do enough to satisfy God. There is the mercenary outlook of those who are always calculating their own merits, measuring their progress, waiting for God to reward them for their efforts, and complaining when things don't go as they think they should. There is the superficial attitude of those who think they've done it all just as soon as they do a little bit of good, and get discouraged or rebel when faced with their limitations. Or the narrow-mindedness of those who measure everything according to strict rules, "weak and beggarly elemental spirits," [9] "human precepts and doctrines," [10] "Do not handle, Do not taste, Do not touch," [11] and make life impossible for others by their merciless legalism or perfectionism.

Taking our stand on the law leads to death, because pride, despair, legalism, calculation, and the rest kill love. Taking our stand on grace leads to life, because it enables love to grow, expand, and flourish. Grace is given freely, and this free giving is the only law under which love can exist. Jesus says: "You received without pay, give without pay." [12] God's love is absolutely free: we don't have to

[9] Galatians 4: 9.
[10] Colossians 2: 22.
[11] Colossians 2: 21.
[12] Matthew 10: 8.

merit it or win it, we only have to receive and welcome it by faith. This is the only path to salvation, according to St. Paul.

Living according to grace is the remedy for pride. We realize that our works are not our own but are what God gives us the grace to do.[13] This is also the remedy for despair, because no matter how terrible our failures, we are never doomed to inevitable damnation—we can always return to God's absolutely free and unconditional love.

Taking our stand on the law, by contrast, prevents us from tasting the glorious freedom of God's children, who know that they are loved unconditionally, independently of their merits and their good or bad grades.

## 4. LEARNING TO LOVE: GIVING AND RECEIVING FREELY

We have been placed on earth to learn to love in the school of Jesus. Learning to love is extremely simple: it means learning to *give freely* and *receive freely*. But this simple lesson also is very hard for us learn, because of sin.

It doesn't come naturally to us to *give freely*. We have a strong tendency to give in order to receive in return. The gift of ourselves is always motivated to some extent by self-gratification. Jesus invites us to escape this limitation and practice a love as pure and disinterested as God's own

---

[13] St. Paul speaks of "good works that God prepared beforehand that we should walk in them," Ephesians 2: 10.

love. "Love your enemies, and do good, and lend, expecting nothing in return; and your reward will be great, and you will be sons of the Most High; for he is kind to the ungrateful and the selfish. Be merciful, even as your Father is merciful. . . ." [14]

Nor do we find it easy to *receive freely*. We are happy to receive something seen as in some way a reward for our merits, something due us. Receiving freely means trusting the giver, with open hearts. It also means abandoning ourselves! And it requires a lot of humility. We can claim things as a right, demand things, but seldom can we receive and accept freely.

We commit a fault against this free giving and receiving, in our relationship with God or with other people, every time we make the good we've done into an excuse for claiming a right, demanding gratitude or recompense. But we also do that more subtly every time we are afraid of not receiving love due to this or that limitation or personal shortcoming. Jesus in the Gospel does all he can to destroy that way of thinking. [15] We find it hard to accept this reversal of our values, but we will never find happiness without it.

Learning to give and receive freely requires a long, laborious process of re-educating our minds, which have

---

[14] Luke 6: 35–36.

[15] For example, he reminds us that we are useless servants (Luke 17: 10), but also says that the workers of the eleventh hour receive the same payment as those of the first hour (Matthew 20: 1–6).

been conditioned by thousands of years of struggle for survival.[16] The violent entry of divine revelation and the Gospel into the world is like an evolutionary ferment, intended to make our psychology "evolve" toward an attitude of free giving and free receiving—the attitude of the Kingdom because it is the attitude of love. This is a process of divinization, whose final goal is to love as God loves: "You must be perfect, as your Father in heaven is perfect."[17] And this divinization, this becoming God-like, means becoming human in the truest sense! It is a marvelous, liberating evolution: but we can only enter into the new way of being through the destruction of many of our natural behaviors, a sort of death-agony. Having entered through the "narrow gate" of this conversion of outlook, however, we find ourselves in a splendid place: the Kingdom, the world where love is the only law, a paradise of free giving and free receiving. Here are no more "rights" and "duties," nothing to defend or earn, no more opposition between "yours" and "mine." Here the heart can expand infinitely.

---

[16] As a matter of fact, despite our technological progress, our psychological makeup could still be termed that of prehistoric man, i.e., it is largely structured around survival, defense, and other mechanisms, so it adapts with difficulty to relationships of trust and disinterested, freely given love. The operation of the Holy Spirit might be described as a work that aims to restructure our psychology to render it able to function in this new mode. The opposition St. Paul draws between the "natural" man and the spiritual man, the "old" man and the new man, could be interpreted in these terms.

[17] Matthew 5: 48.

V

# SPIRITUAL POVERTY
# AND FREEDOM

## I. THE NEED TO BE

One of man's deepest needs is the need for identity.[1] We need to know who we are; we need to exist in our own eyes and other people's. That need for identity is so strong that it can lead to aberrations. We see this particularly today, when men and women, especially young people, can adapt the most bizarre "look" dictated by current fads, simply as a way of asserting that they are who they are. The media offer many different models: the young, dynamic executive, the sports star, the super-model, the street-smart kid. . . .

[1] At the psychological and spiritual level, man's deepest need is the need for love: the need to love and to be loved. Two other basic needs are necessarily linked to this need for love and communion: the need for truth (in order to love, we need to know); and the need for identity (in order to love, we need to be). These three basic needs correspond to the three spiritual faculties that theology traditionally identifies in man: will, intellect, and memory. The theological virtues enable us to find the ultimate satisfaction of these needs in God himself: faith gives us access to the truth, hope enables us to find our security and identity in God, and charity makes us live in communion of love with God and our neighbor.

At the most superficial level, this need for identity often seeks satisfaction in material possessions and a certain external lifestyle: we identify ourselves with our riches, our physical appearance, our motorbike or yacht. This is terribly confused: we are trying to satisfy a need for *being* by *having*. It may keep us happy for a while, but that doesn't last and disappointments soon come. Realizing that the only thing others were interested in was their money, not themselves, people experience a terrible loneliness.

At a slightly higher level, the need to *be* seeks satisfaction through acquiring and exercising certain talents, whether sporting, artistic, or intellectual. There is then a risk of confusing *being* with *doing.* But what if someone loses his or her collection of talents and abilities? Suppose the world-class football player ends up in a wheelchair? Suppose the man who knows French literature backward and forward loses his memory in an accident? Who are they then?

It is normal and good to discover that one can do such and such a thing, actualize one's potential, and so learn who one is. Thus we acquire self-confidence and experience the joy of expressing the talents entrusted to us. Our upbringing and education are, as they should be, largely based on this tendency.

But identity is not rooted in the sum of one's aptitudes. Individuals have a unique value and dignity, independently of what they can *do*. Someone who doesn't realize this is at risk of having a real "identity crisis" on the day he or she experiences failure, or of despising others when faced with their limitations. Where is there room for the poor and the handicapped in a world where people are measured by their efficiency and the profit they can produce?

### 2. PRIDE AND SPIRITUAL POVERTY

Here it is worth reflecting on the problem of pride.[2] We are all born with a deep wound, experienced as a lack of being. We seek to compensate by constructing a self different from our real self. This artificial self requires large amounts of energy to maintain it; being fragile, it needs protecting. Woe to anyone who contradicts it, threatens it, questions it, or inhibits its expansion. When the Gospel says we must "die to ourselves," it means this artificial ego, this constructed self, must die, so that the real "self" given us by God can emerge.

This same tendency also exists in our spiritual lives. It is normal and positive, a source of human and spiritual growth, since it motivates us to progress, to acquire gifts and talents, to imitate this or that model. Wanting to be someone like St. Francis of Assisi or Mother Teresa can set us off on the path of holiness.

But this becomes a dangerous problem if we stop at that point. Obviously, it is excellent to do good things

[2] These reflections are taken from an article by Brother Ephraïm in *Ressources d'eau vive*, a journal of Christian psychology produced under the auspices of the Communauté des Béatitudes, Nouan-le-Fuzelier, France.

such as prayer, fasting, devoting ourselves to the service of our neighbor, evangelizing, and so on. But it is extremely dangerous to *identify ourselves with the spiritual good we are able to do*. For this identity is still an artificial and fragile one that will collapse on the day one of our virtues fails or a particular spiritual talent into which we had poured our whole selves is taken from us. How can we endure failures, if we identify ourselves with our spiritual successes? I have met religious who gave their all in the apostolate, devoting themselves body and soul to a good cause, and who, on the day sickness or the decision of a superior obliged them to cease, experienced a profound crisis to the point of no longer knowing who they were.

Identification of the self with the good one is able to accomplish leads to spiritual pride: consciously or not, we consider ourselves the source of that good, instead of recognizing that all the good we are able to do is a free gift from God. "What have you that you did not receive? If then you received it, why do you boast as if it were not a gift?" [3] This pride leads us to pass judgment on those who do not accomplish as much as we do, to be impatient with those who prevent us from carrying out a given project, and so forth.

Pride, hardheartedness, contempt for neighbor, along with fear and discouragement are the inevitable results of confusing my *self* with my *talents*. Failures are unendur-

[3] 1 Corinthians 4: 7.

able, because instead of being seen as normal, even beneficial, they are perceived as an attack on our being.

Human beings are more than the sum of the good they can accomplish. They are children of God, whether they do good or cannot yet manage to do anything. Our Father in heaven does not love us because of the good we do. He loves us for ourselves, because he has adopted us as his children forever. [4]

This is why humility, spiritual poverty, is so precious: it locates our identity securely in the one place where it will be safe from all harm. If our treasure is in God, no one can take it from us. Humility is truth. I am what I am in God's eyes: a poor child who possesses absolutely nothing, who receives everything, infinitely loved and totally free. I have received everything in advance from the freely bestowed love of my Father, who said to me definitively: "All that is mine is yours." [5]

Our treasure is not the kind that moths or worms can devour.[6] It is in heaven in God's hands. It depends on God alone, his good will and unfailing goodness to us. Our identity has its source in the creative love of God, who made us in his own image and destines us to live with him forever.

---

[4] Here is the key to the well-known "midlife crisis." People find in their fifties that they have a great inner emptiness, because they wanted to live by doing, while forgetting their true, inalienable identity as children of God, loved not for what they do but what they are.

[5] Luke 15: 31.

[6] Matthew 6: 19.

Love is what remains when nothing remains. We all carry within us this memory when, beyond our failures, our separations, the words we survived, there arises from the depths of the night, like a song that is barely audible, the assurance that beyond the disasters in our lives, even beyond joy, suffering, birth, death, there exists a space where nothing threatens, that nothing has ever threatened and that runs no risk of destruction, an intact space, that of the love that was the foundation of our being.[7]

This does not mean it doesn't matter whether we behave well or badly. We should do good and avoid evil as far as we can, because sin hurts God, harms us, and harms other people, and the damage it causes is often difficult to put right. But we have no right to identify people with the wrong they do. That would be to imprison them and lose all hope in their regard. Nor can we identify anyone—especially not ourselves—with the good they do.

### 3. SPIRITUAL TRIALS

These considerations shed light on the way God teaches and trains us individually, and on the meaning of trials in the spiritual life.

The trials or "purifications" so frequently referred to

[7] Christiane Singer, *Du bon usage des crises*, p. 79.

by the mystics are there to destroy whatever is artificial in our character, so that our true being may emerge—i.e., what we are to God. The night of the soul could be called a series of impoverishments, sometimes violent ones, that strip believers of all possibility of relying on themselves. These trials are beneficial, because they lead us to locate our identity where it truly belongs. The experience can be highly painful when someone who loves God goes through a phase without an atom of fervor and even with a profound distaste for spiritual things. People do not lose their love for God, for their whole being remains completely oriented toward God; but they lose the feeling of love. The benefit of this trial that it deprives us of any possibility of relying on the good we can do. God's mercy is all. A priest once told me in confession: "When you no longer believe in what you can do for God, continue believing in what God can do for you."

Progressively, and in a way that parallels their terrible impoverishment, those who go through such trials while still hoping in the Lord, begin to realize the truth of something that up until then was only a pious expression: God loves us in an absolutely unconditional way, by virtue of himself, his mercy, and his infinite tenderness, by virtue of his Fatherhood toward us.

This experience produces a fundamental change in our Christian lives. It is an immense grace. The basis of our relationship to God no longer lies in us but wholly and exclusively in God. Now we become fully free. When our relationship to God has God's fatherhood as its only foundation, it is safe from all harm.

People who have passed through this sort of trial are more than ever in love with God and wish to please him by good works, but the good they do is done purely, freely, and disinterestedly. It does not proceed from a need to create an identity or a thirst for success. Nor does it have the hidden motive of wanting a reward. Its source is God.

This spiritual conversion well described by the Egyptian monk Matta El-Maskeen or el Maskine (Matthew the Poor) in his work on prayer.

> When Christians devote themselves to the spiritual combat, to assiduousness in prayer and the careful observance of other spiritual practices, they can come to feel that this activity and this assiduousness condition their relationship with God. It seems to them then that it is by reason of their perseverance and fidelity to prayers that they deserve to be loved by God and become His children. But God does not want souls to go astray down that false path, which would, in fact, separate them for good from God's freely bestowed love, and life with Him. So He takes away the energy and assiduousness that threaten them with this loss.

> Once God has taken away the abilities that He had offered freely in proof of His love—these souls

are left without strength, incapable of performing any spiritual action, and are confronted with the stupefying truth that they resist believing and persist in seeing as highly improbable: God in His fatherhood does not need our prayers and our good works. At the beginning, they cling to the idea that God has withdrawn His fatherly care from them after they stopped praying; and that God has abandoned them and neglects them because their works and perseverance were not up to the measure of their love. They try in vain to get up from their prostration and mourning and take up their former activity, but all his resolutions go for nothing. And then, little by little, they begin to understand that God's greatness is not to be measured by the yardstick of man's futility, that His eminently superior fatherhood chose to adopt the children of dust because of His infinite tenderness and the immensity of His grace, and not in return for the works of man or our efforts; that our adoption by God is a truth that has its source in God and not in ourselves, a truth that is ever present, that persists—in spite of our powerlessness and our sin—in witnessing to God's goodness and His generosity. In this way, their spiritual lukewarmness leads these souls to revise their concept of God fundamentally, and also their evaluation of the spiritual relations between the soul and God. This profoundly modifies their concept of effort and assiduousness in spiritual works. They no longer consider these things as the price of God's love, but as responses to His love and fatherly care.[8]

What God does in the souls of certain people by plunging them into that sort of "spiritual lukewarmness" is something he would like to do to everyone, though perhaps in a less extraordinary and more gradual way, by means of their sufferings: failure, helplessness, falls of every kind, sickness, depression, psychological and affective weaknesses, even if they are our own fault. There is no great difference between spiritual trials and other trials. God makes use of everything, even the consequences of our sins! It is consoling to know that we can draw great spiritual profit from a trial with nothing spiritual about it.

### 4. RELYING ON MERCY ALONE

"Mature" Christians, who have truly become children of God, are those who have experienced their radical nothingness, their absolute poverty, been reduced to nothing. At the bottom of that nothingness, they have finally discovered the inexpressible tenderness, the absolutely unconditional love, of God. Henceforth their only support and hope is the boundless mercy of their Father God. For

[8] Matta el Maskine, *L'Expérience de Dieu dans la vie de prière* (in the Le Cerf edition, p. 295).

them, the words God speaks to the people of Israel through the prophet Zephaniah have come true: "I will leave in the midst of you a people humble and lowly. They shall seek refuge in the name of the Lord." [9] They do all the good they can. They receive what their neighbor may do for them with joy and gratitude, but in great freedom, because their support is in God alone. They are untroubled by their own weaknesses, nor do they blame others for not always meeting their expectations. Reliance on God alone protects them from all disappointment. It gives them great interior freedom, which they place entirely at the service of God and their fellow men, responding to love with love.

## 5. THE TRULY FREE PERSON IS THE ONE WHO HAS NOTHING LEFT TO LOSE

The world seeks freedom in the accumulation of possessions and power. It forgets that the only people who are truly free are those who have nothing left to lose. Despoiled of everything, detached from everything, they are "free from all men" [10] and all things. It can be truly said that their death is already behind them, because all their "treasure" is now in God and in him alone. The people who are supremely free desire nothing and are afraid of nothing. All the good that matters to them is already guaranteed them by God. They have nothing to lose and nothing to

[9] Zephaniah 3: 12.
[10] St. Paul uses this expression in 1 Corinthians 9: 19.

defend. These are the "poor in spirit" of the Beatitudes, detached, humble, merciful, meek, peacemakers.

There is a parable expressing this truth in Solzhenitsyn's book *The First Circle*, which is set in the era of Stalin's dictatorship. A highly placed party official needs the services of a "zek", who is a scientist, for a project he has been put in charge of and on which he is risking his career. He presents all possible arguments to persuade him to collaborate. Solzhenitsyn shows perceptively how the really free man in this exchange is not the powerful official but the prisoner, because he has nothing left to lose. He is ready to go back to Siberia if necessary: even in those terrible conditions one can still be a man.

Gulags and concentration camps were one of the greatest traumas of the twentieth century, yet they provided abundant cases of people who found true freedom behind bars. In her book, Etty Hillesum, imprisoned in the camp at Westerbork, reflects:

> The barbed wire is more a question of attitude.
>
> '*Us* behind barbed wire?' an indestructible old gentleman once said with a melancholy wave of his hand. '*They* are the ones who live behind barbed wire'—and he pointed to the tall villas that stand like sentries on the other side of the fence.[11]

[11] Hillesum, *Interrupted Life*, p. 299.

She also writes: "If you have a rich interior life, I would have said, there probably isn't all that much difference between the inside and outside of a [prison] camp." [12]

### 6. HAPPY ARE THE POOR

As the years go by, I meet people with whom I share things at a deep level and experience the quiet, mysterious, but very real action of God in my life and theirs. More and more I am struck by the wisdom in the Gospel and by the way the Word throws astonishingly accurate light on the human condition. This paradoxical, inexhaustible Gospel has unheard-of power to "humanize" us.

At the center of the Gospel stand the Beatitudes. The first one sums up all the others: "Blessed are the poor in spirit, for theirs is the Kingdom of Heaven." I hope this book has helped the reader to understand this astonishing statement by Jesus and begin to put it into practice. Spiritual poverty, utter dependence on God and his mercy, is the condition for interior freedom. We need to become children and "consent to expect everything as a gift from God our Father: absolutely everything, moment by moment." [13]

We don't know what events will mark the third millennium, but one thing is certain: those who have learned to

[12] Hillesum, *Interrupted Life*, p. 107.
[13] Jean-Claude Sagne, *Viens vers le Père*, p. 172.

discover and expand the inalienable space of freedom that God placed in their hearts by making them his children, will never be caught off guard.

By way of conclusion, I offer for the reader's meditation a beautiful dialogue between Jesus and a contemporary Spanish spiritual writer, who has had a close relationship with our Lady since childhood and who has chosen to remain anonymous.

"Have you never wondered which of all the things you experience causes me the greatest joy?"

"No," I said to Jesus.

He answered, "When, in lucid freedom, you say yes to God's calls." And then he continued, "Remember what it says in the Gospel, 'The truth will make you free.' You can only respond freely to the calls of grace when your own truth becomes clear, when you accept it humbly, and when, on that basis, you maintain a conversation with God, realizing that everything that has happened and happens to you is part of a loving and providential project of your Father God.

"Yes, many things will cause you perplexity. They will even plunge you into intense darkness and, still more, into suffering that wounds and paralyzes you. But if you have recourse to your faith, it will be your shield. Doesn't God reveal himself as your *Abba*? Have not I, the Son, taken on your condition at it's most wretched? Doesn't the Paraclete defend you? Believe all this with heart and soul, and it will fill you with trust and confidence.

"Don't be afraid of yourselves! Don't be afraid of all that you are, in your human reality, where God pitches his tent to dwell with you. God is incarnation. God's new name is Emmanuel, God with us: God with your reality. Open yourself to it without fear. Only in the measure you discover yourself will you discover the depths of his love. In the depths of what you are, you will experience that you are not alone. Someone, lovingly and mercifully, has entered into the mystery of your humanity, not as spectator, not as judge, but as someone who loves you, who offers himself to you, who espouses you to free you, save you, and heal you. . . . To stay with you forever, loving you, loving you!"

Easter, 2002